Blood on the Streets

The Civil War Comes to

Jackson County, Missouri,

August 1862

By Ralph A. Monaco, II

Blood on the Streets

The Civil War Comes to Jackson County, Missouri, August 1862

By Ralph A. Monaco, II

Civil War Sesquicentennial Series

Jackson County Historical Society
Monaco Publishing, LLC
Independence, Missouri

2012

© 2012, Ralph A. Monaco, II

Monaco, Ralph A. (1956-)
 Blood on the Streets: Civil War Comes to Jackson County, Missouri, August 1862 /
  By Ralph A Monaco, II.
  94 pages. Includes Bibliography and Index.

ISBN-13: 978-0974136585 (Jackson County Historical Society)
ISBN-10: 0-9741365-8-1

1. Jackson County (Mo.)—History—Civil War, 1861-1865. 2. Missouri—History—Civil War, 1861-1865. 3. West (U.S.)—History—Civil War, 1861-1865. I. Monaco, Ralph A. (1956-) author. II. Title.

First Edition, December 2012

Published in the United States of America by:

Monaco Publishing, LLC
c/o Jackson County Historical Society
P.O. Box 4241
Independence, MO 64051-4241
816.252.7454
info@jchs.org
www.jchs.org

TABLE OF CONTENTS

vi

DEDICATION

To My Wife Karen

for her patience in accepting my countless hours

of burning of the midnight oil while writing history

&

for her sense of humor in tolerating

my donning of 19th century wardrobe as a living historian

PREFACE

Prelude to War

The bombardment of Fort Sumter in the harbor of Charleston, South Carolina, by Confederates under General Pierre Gustave Toutant Beauregard in the early morning hours of April 12, 1861, was not the beginning of hostilities between the north and south. By the time the shelling had commenced and before Major Robert Anderson had surrendered the fort, the Civil War had been raging along the Missouri-Kansas Border for nearly seven years. Following the adoption of the Kansas-Nebraska Act, signed into law by President Franklin Pierce on May 30, 1854, the seminal issue confronting the United States was the extension of slavery into the Territories of Nebraska and Kansas. Most Missourians were convinced that Kansas would enter the Union as a slave state and Nebraska as a free state. Their logic and reasoning was predicated upon the belief that this alignment would continue to assure the balance of free and slave states in the Congress at Washington City.[1] Abolitionists and those opposed to the extension of the peculiar institution were as equally determined to ensure that both territories would enter the Union as free-states.

The term "Bleeding Kansas" in the mid- to late-1850s was not mere words; it was a reality. While partisan debates raged in the halls of Congress and in local and national newspapers, blood flowed in Kansas. As the Supreme Court considered arguments and entered its holding enjoining Congressional authority to restrict slavery's expansion, nothing curtailed the thunder on the border. Boundary lines were challenged and contested. Battles were fought and waged. Lives were lost and sacrificed. Property was seized and destroyed. Bitterness mounted and intensified. And, lawlessness and criminality reigned. Horror dominated the Missouri-Kansas border and Jackson County.

By the time Abraham Lincoln was elected President of the United States in November 1860, the nation's fabric was being

---

[1] The Nation's Capitol was known as Washington City before, during and after the Civil War. It did not become known as Washington, D.C. until the 1890's.

1

torn and ripped to shreds over the issue of slavery. Southern states were convinced that Lincoln's election meant the destruction of slavery, thereby necessitating secession from the Union. South Carolina led the way. Northerners were divided between those who anxiously desired to fight to preserve the Union to those willing to allow the South to depart freely and without intervention. The sentiment in Missouri was as equally diverse and split. St. Louis and its large population of German immigrants held firm to the Union. Communities along the Missouri and Mississippi River Valley remained steadfast to their predominantly southern cultural heritage. Jackson County continued to experience the same political division and emotional instability that it had struggled with throughout the years of "Bleeding Kansas."

Votes cast by Missourians during the fall election of 1860 are demonstrative of the divided sentiment within the state. While the state's electoral votes went to Illinois Senator Steven Douglas, the "Little Giant," it was not an overwhelming victory. Senator John Bell of Tennessee, an anti-secessionist and Unconditional Unionist, finished a close second. Vice-President John Breckenridge had campaigned under his splintered Democratic

Party's platform that was fully committed to the preservation of states' rights, and especially the southern slaveholding cause. Breckenridge finished a distant third in the presidential balloting. Lincoln ran last in the election. While he garnered his chief support from the German population in St. Louis, Lincoln had fared poorly in the western side of the state. Lincoln did not receive a single vote in Clay County, and only a handful in Jackson County.

This divisiveness in Missouri was further demonstrated by the gubernatorial election. The two leading candidates for that office were Democrat Claiborne Fox Jackson and Sample Orr of Springfield, Greene County. Jackson was a resident of mid-Missouri, who was deeply committed to the southern agrarian way of life. During the fall campaign, Jackson had publicly endorsed Douglas and his fervent dedication to the preservation of the Union. Orr ran as an Unconditional

Claiborne Fox Jackson

Unionist and publicly articulated his opposition to secession. The Republican candidate was James B. Gardenhire. His party had placed him on the ballot knowing full-well that he had no possibility of winning the race. Jackson won the governor's race but only by a marginal vote. Jackson received 47% of the votes cast to Orr's forty-two percent.

While Jackson had campaigned under the mantle of Senator Douglas, the actions he took following his election as governor compared to the politics of Breckenridge. In Governor Jackson's inaugural address, given after several southern states had seceded from the Union, he emphatically declared:

"The first drop of bloodshed in a war of aggression upon a sovereign State will arouse a spirit which must result in the overthrow of our entire Federal system, and which this generation will never see quelled . . . The destiny of the slave-holding States of this Union is one and the same. So long as a State continues to maintain slavery within her limits, it is impossible to separate her fate from that of her sister States."

In other words, his commitment was to the southern states and their "cause." Jackson's speech went on to include a request of the Missouri Legislature to enact legislation creating a new state militia and calling for a Constitutional Convention to be convened at the State Capitol in Jefferson City in February 1861. The purpose for convening the convention, Jackson argued, was to determine the relationship between Missouri and the Union. The Missouri Legislature acted promptly to Governor Jackson's requests. The General Assembly passed a law that called for the election of three delegates from each of the state's 33 senatorial districts. This gave St. Louis, the eighth largest city in the country with a population in excess of 160,000, the largest delegation. St. Louis would have a total of 15 representatives serving at the Convention.

On Monday, February 17, voters assembled throughout the state to elect delegates to the State's Constitutional Convention. The election did not go the way in which the Governor and his strident supporters had anticipated. Much to Governor Jackson's surprise and dismay, Missouri voters overwhelmingly, and by some 80,000 votes elected pro-union, anti-secessionist delegates.

Jackson and his advocates should not have been astonished by this outcome. The largest majority of the presidential votes cast in Missouri had gone to Senator Douglas and Senator Bell, both of whom were in open opposition to secession and were ardent Union men. Likewise, a large majority of Missourians during the preceding November's gubernatorial election had gone to candidates opposed to secession. Voters in the 14th Senatorial District compromising Jackson County and Cass County voted with the majority. They elected Abram Comingo of Independence;[2] Robert A. Brown, a large slaveholder from

---

[2] Abram Comingo was born in Harrodsburg, Kentucky in January 1820. In 1848, he and his wife, Lucy, and his law partner, William Chrisman, and his wife, Lucy Lee Chrisman, emigrated to Independence. Comingo served two terms as Mayor of Independence in the 1850s. After he voted for the Union during the Constitutional Convention in 1861, he was appointed Provost Marshal for the 6th Congressional District in 1863. He had the bitter assignment of enforcing General Ewing's Order #11. Following the Civil War, Comingo, in 1866, was elected as the First Recorder of Deeds of Jackson County. In 1870, he was elected to Congress to represent Jackson County in the U.S. House of Representatives where he served two terms. In 1883 his law firm, Philips, Comingo & Slover, had successfully defended Frank James in Davies County, Missouri, for the 1881 Winston train robbery. He passed away in Kansas City in

Harrisonville, Cass County; and, James K. Shelley, Judge of the Court of Common Pleas in Independence and Kansas City, to represent the District at the Convention. In all, 99 delegates from every corner of the state comprised the delegation of the Convention.

When the delegates to the Constitutional Convention assembled in Jefferson City on February 28, they soon realized several problems with the convention being held at the State Capitol. First, the city lacked sufficient boarding facilities. More disturbing, however, was the discovery that the city was a hotbed of unrest and secessionist sentiment. Located on the southern bank of the Missouri River, the capitol city had long been associated with the mid-Missouri River southern planter, pro-slavery culture and mindset. It was unquestioned that the fervor in the area was tilting towards secession from the Union.

Given this climate, a decision was made by the end of the second day's session to relocate the convention to St. Louis—a venue considered much more adapted to the body's Union outlook.

Day three opened on Monday, March 4, in the Merchants Library Hall located on the second floor of the south wing of the Circuit Courthouse in St. Louis. (This was the same day in which Abraham Lincoln gave his inaugural address in Washington City as the 16th President of the United States.)

The re-location of the Constitutional Convention was successful. Fifty-one-year-old Sterling Price, former Governor of Missouri (1853-1857), former General during the Mexican War (1846-1848), and a large plantation and slave owner from mid-Missouri, was elected President of the Convention. After several days of debate, the convention delegates on Tuesday, March 19 (the 16th day of their deliberation) almost unanimously voted against secession. In a vote of 89-1 the assembly found no basis or adequate cause to dissolve the state's relationship with the Federal Union.

The three delegates elected from the 14th Senatorial District (including Jackson County) was no exception; they, too, voted with the vast majority. Even the President of the Convention,

---

November 1889 at the age of 69.

5

Sterling Price, cast his support for the Union.

Fifty-one-year-old George Y. Bast, a physician and farmer who had been born in Kentucky and who had moved with his parents to the Missouri River Valley in Montgomery County, cast the lone negative vote. His background and nativity had been part of a slave holding culture, and his genealogy and heritage explained his vote and his support to the sentiments towards secession.

Although the Convention had almost unanimously opposed any movement towards secession, this did not mean that the State of Missouri would not continue to suffer strife and discord over the issue. There were too many people in the state who had been born in slave holding states who continued to hold firm to their roots and maintained a pronounced, dedicated loyalty to their sister states in the South.

Only the test of time and bloodshed would determine the true outcome of whether Missouri would remain within the Union.

CHAPTER I

War Comes to Missouri—An Overview, 1861

Following the attack on Fort Sumter, President Lincoln issued a proclamation calling for 75,000 volunteers from the several states in order to put down the rebellion. Missouri Governor Claiborne Fox Jackson was incensed by the President's request. He promptly declared that the State of Missouri would not furnish a single troop *"to subjugate her sister states of the South."* He further called out the state militia to assemble in St. Louis and convened the Missouri General Assembly into special session. While the special legislative session met in Jefferson City, the State Guard under Brigadier General Daniel M. Frost gathered in St. Louis at Camp Jackson, named in tribute to the Governor.[3] Under the Constitution of Missouri, the assemblage of the militia was legal and constitutional. Similar militia musters were being held throughout the state likewise in accordance to the constitution.

The Federal government, fearing that Governor Jackson's militia intended to capture the Federal armory in St. Louis, took immediate steps to quash the militia. Captain Nathaniel Lyon, a Connecticut native, graduate of West Point, and Mexican War veteran, had been recently re-assigned from Fort Riley, Kansas to St. Louis. Lyon was known to be an uncompromising soul and an overt, unrelenting zealot. While he was not an abolitionist, he had openly opposed slavery's expansion and he had experienced much of the military and civil discord during the years in which blood spilled over the Kansas-Missouri Border, having been assigned to Fort Riley in 1855. Lyon was known to be an avid Unionist who detested secession, or for that matter, anyone who disagreed with his views or opinions on any topic. The experience he had garnered in dealing with Missouri pro-slavery advocates during the days of

---

[3] Frost had graduated from West Point in 1844 and had served in the Mexican War. After he resigned his army commission in 1853, he engaged in the lumber and fur business in St. Louis and served four years in the Missouri Senate. Frost was serving as the Brigadier General of the Missouri militia at the time the militia muster was being held at Camp Jackson in St. Louis.

BLOOD ON THE STREETS

'Bleeding Kansas" had taught him the necessity of prompt and unequivocal action in proceeding against "border ruffians." Lyon had justification to consider Frost to be one of the leading members of the anti-Union sentiment in Missouri, and specifically within St. Louis.

With this background, Lyon took decisive action. He was well aware that southern sympathizers in Liberty, Missouri, earlier in April, had seized the Federal arsenal. Lyon was not going to permit this happen in St. Louis. Instead, Lyon immediately took political and military steps and successfully secured the Federal arsenal in St. Louis.

He then turned his attention to Frost and the approximate 1,000 members of the Missouri militia. When Lyon discovered that ammunition, supplies, and cannons from Baton Rouge, Louisiana, had been delivered by the Confederacy to Frost, Lyon once again reacted instantly. Lyon was not going to wait for Frost to have time to unlimber his guns. On May 10, St. Louis Congressman Frank Blair and Lyon ordered their troops to encircle Camp Jackson. Frost had no option and was compelled to surrender and stack arms. Tragedy and bloodshed soon erupted in what has become known as the Camp Jackson Massacre. As Lyon's men marched the beleaguered, captured Missouri State Guard through the streets of St. Louis, those in sympathy with the militia began to vocally criticize Lyon's force—most of who were Germans. Stones and rocks were hurled at Lyon's company; but, when someone fired into the Federal ranks, carnage followed. Lyon's men promptly responded with a barrage of gunfire. When the shooting had ended, blood stained the streets. In total, 28 citizens, two Union soldiers and three militia members were dead. Over 75 others were wounded during the "massacre." Even the following day, bloodshed continued to pour onto the streets of St. Louis as German Home Guard troops fired into rioters killing 11 more civilians. Unrest and mayhem prevailed.

The southern reaction in Missouri to the Camp Jackson tragedy was pronounced. Many residents of St. Louis fled the city fearing further retaliation by the "murdering Dutch." The General Assembly at Jefferson City promptly passed a special military bill giving Governor Jackson near dictatorial power. The Governor further requested funds from the legislature to raise and equip an army. The Missouri Legislature quickly complied by appropriating funds, authorizing loans and issuing bonds for that purpose. In St. Joseph, Mayor M. Jeff Thompson (later to be known during the Civil War as the "Swamp Fox" in southeast Missouri), confiscated wagons to take powder, and led to aid in the southern cause.

Observing the fury across the state following the massacre and bloodletting at Camp Jackson, Governor Jackson and Sterling Price felt it essential to avoid a confrontation with the Federal government. The Governor, along with former Governor Price, attempted to negotiate a "peace" treaty in St. Louis with Captain Lyon and Congressman Blair. Lyon saw their intentions as nothing more than a subterfuge. Lyon gave a monomaniacal proclamation in which he bellowed that he would not concede Missouri to the Governor or his militia. Lyon then summarily declared that a state of war existed between the Federal government and the State of Missouri. Price and Governor Jackson were compelled to immediately leave the city following their failed conference, and returned to the State Capitol. At Jefferson City, the Governor offered to Price the command of the newly created Missouri State Guard. Despite having served as President of the Constitutional Convention and having voted against an ordinance of secession, Price accepted the assignment and became commanding general of the state's military force.

While Missouri never legally seceded from the Union, the first year of the War in the state was complex, volatile, ruthless and bloody. Missouri State Guard troops, under General Price and Governor Jackson, battled Missourians, Kansans and other Federal forces. From Athens in the northeast to Wilson's Creek in the southwest,[4] and from Lexington in Lafayette County to the boot heal region of the state, they fought and warred. Some battles included large armies pitted against each other, while most encounters were turbulent struggles between irregular bands of guerillas and Union and Kansas patrols.

---

[4] Captain Lyons was promoted to the rank of General prior to the Battle of Wilson's Creek (or Battle of Oak Hills to the Confederate troops). During that battle on August 10, 1861 General Lyon was killed in action while leading his Union troops.

9

The gravity of the unrest throughout the state caused the Federal government to usurp--or simply ignore--the municipal or county governments.

As the summer of 1861 waned in Missouri, Federal forces secured and held all the principal towns in the state, including the largest cities in Jackson County: Kansas City, Westport and the County Seat at Independence.

Delegates at the state's Constitutional Convention returned in special session and immediately endorsed the actions taken by the Federal government. They vacated the offices of governor, lieutenant governor, secretary of state, and the general assembly. They appointed Hamilton Rowan Gamble as Provisional Governor of the State, and Jackson County resident, artist, and politician, George Caleb Bingham, was named the Provisional State Treasurer.

By the end of 1861, Union forces had forced the Missouri State Guard into winter encampment in Arkansas.

Jim Lane

The State of Missouri, including Jackson County, would for the next four years suffer under the restraints, restrictions, regulations and rules of martial law and the military dictates of the Federal government and its local commanding provost marshals.

The 1861 turmoil in Missouri also rekindled the fire of the Border War years with Kansas. In January 1861, Kansas Territory became the 34th state admitted into the Union. The bloody struggle over slavery in Kansas had ended with its admission as a free state. However, statehood did not end any of the past loathing, or alter any of the prior resentments Kansas residents held for Missouri . . . and especially Jackson County.

The recently elected United States Senator from Kansas, James

Henry "Jim" Lane, wasted no time in seeking to fan the flames of the previous seven years. Under his leadership, he and other Kansas radicals remained as determined as ever to chastise Missourians, whether or not they provided aid, succor or support to the southern cause. Lane insisted that his troops should enter Missouri and destroy anything that was disloyal, *"from a Shanghai rooster to a Durham cow."*

Kansas troops, many without Federal authority, complied with Senator's Lane's edict. Senator Lane was not one to merely articulate words; but, he was willing to back his comments with his own action and wrath. On September 22, bearing the title of U.S. Senator and Brigadier General, Lane marched his forces unmolested into the town of Osceola, Missouri, St. Clair County Seat. They burned Osceola to the ground and left its population of around 2,500 homeless.

In Westport, in Jackson County, there were countless stories of how Jayhawkers harassed citizens and stole property.

The county seat of Jackson County was not to be overlooked by the marauding efforts of the Kansas forces. In November 1861, Colonel Charles "Doc" Jennison of the 7th Regiment of Kansas Volunteers was stationed at Kansas City. He and his Kansans soon set their eyes on Independence. While traveling east to the County Seat, Jennison's men scorched the homes along the route. Thereafter they marched uninterrupted into

Independence. Jennison promptly seized the town and ordered the arrest and corralling of the male residents into the public square. Jennison interrogated the men assembled until only those of southern sentiment remained. He then read a proclamation in which he warned that for every Union soldier killed he would retaliate by killing 10 southerners. Jennison then authorized his force to ransack and loot stores and shops. At least one home was destroyed by fire set by Jennison's men.

After inflicting their wrath and punishment upon Independence, Jennison's men set their sights on Westport, located within one mile of the Kansas border. George Caleb Bingham reported that the route taken by Jennison's troops from Independence to Westport could be traced by devastation. He declared that all that remained in the wake of Jennison's march westward were the ruins of the homes that were first indiscriminately pillaged, and then burned. A young William Wallace (who later prosecuted Frank James in 1882 and 1883) told how Captain Pardee of Col. Jennison's 7th Cavalry came to his parent's property in Jackson County and sacked their home and took everything of value that could be carried off their land.

These persistent and destructive activities of Jennison, Lane, and others including, James Montgomery, a former disciple of John Brown during the bleeding days of Kansas, resulted in

outright devastation to Jackson County. The prowling Kansas troops arbitrarily burned farms and crops, wantonly seized large quantities of chattel and other personal property and senselessly committed murders. Jackson County had become a desolate and ravaged area where solitude reigned supreme and terror filled the hearts and souls of those who remained. Countless other towns in Missouri suffered the same fate as Jackson County. For example, on the

George Caleb Bingham

morning of New Year's Day 1862, Kansas troops under Dan Anthony (the brother of suffragette Susan B. Anthony) captured the town of Dayton, Cass County and then burned it to the ground.

The ruthlessness by which these Kansas troops behaved along the western border of Missouri, including Jackson County, had certain long-term negative consequences. General Price opined that the best recruiters for the southern cause had been the actions and privations caused and inflicted upon Missouri by these Kansans. The Federal government equally shared Price's poignant remark. Major General Henry Halleck, the commanding general of the Department of the West stationed in St. Louis, declared that the conduct of Lane and Jennison in western Missouri and Jackson County had turned thousands of former Union men against the government. In the end, Jennison and many other Kansas Jayhawkers and Red Legs were re-assigned and removed from the border district in an attempt to prevent them from inflicting further pain and turmoil to the region. They were sent as far away as possible from the area and they were dispatched to battle Confederate forces east of Mississippi River.

BLOOD ON THE STREETS

CHAPTER II

Southern Recruitment in Jackson County, 1862

By the end of 1861, residents of Jackson County had experienced just the beginning of a ruthless and irregular conflict that would be filled with criminality on both sides in which families, friends and former associates were pitted against one another.

The first large Civil War engagement in 1862 took place on March 7 and 8 in northwestern Arkansas in what has become known as the Battle of Pea Ridge (or, Elkhorn Tavern to southerners). Missouri State Guard troops under the command of General Sterling Price were joined and united by troops under General James McIntosh from Arkansas and General Ben McCullough of Texas. Over a two-day period, Union forces under General Sam Curtis fought a hotly contested battle against the combined Confederate and State Guard troops from Missouri. The conflict proved to be a Union victory and summarily ended the military career of the Missouri State Guard. Following their defeat at Pea Ridge, a number of members of the State Guard, including Price, were mustered into the Confederate Army and were sent east to the Trans-Mississippi Valley. However, an equal percentage of the former guard members chose not to enlist in the Confederacy. Instead, they decided to return to their beleaguered homes in Missouri and Jackson County. The loss at Pea Ridge did not symbolize the end to Southern attempts to regain support within the State of Missouri. Confederate leaders realized that the state continued to offer fertile ground for the recruitment of southern men into their ranks. Confederates were further assured that sentiments in western Missouri remained in support of their "cause." **Upton Hays** of Jackson County among others were given commissions in the Confederate Army and dispatched into

Missouri to recruit troops. Colonel Upton Hays and many other Confederate officers had experienced first-hand the terror inflicted upon western Missouri by Kansas troops. They also knew that the atrocities committed by Jayhawkers and Red Legs had made Jackson County a breeding ground for enlistments.[5]

The violence that the Kansan troops had inflicted upon the county was not the only basis for the south to be encouraged about the potential for volunteers. All residents of Missouri had been ordered and compelled to sign a loyalty oath to the Federal government or post a bond to ensure their good conduct. Equally and perhaps even more disheartening than the loyalty oath and bond requirements was the mandate issued by Governor Gamble in the late spring of 1862. The Governor had issued a proclamation in which all Missouri men of lawful age, between the ages of 18 and 45 were compelled to join the militia in aid of the Union. This decree proved to be the final tonic and incentive for men to enlist in the Confederate Army (or, to join one of the various guerilla units, including those under Captain William Clarke Quantrill, who had been operating within Jackson County).

The Governor's order further emboldened Quantrill and his men. They began to run "wild" in Jackson County. They ambushed border towns in Kansas, seized United States Mail escorts, and

---

[5] In 2011, Ms. Marian Franklin and family donated The Watts and Hays Family Letters Collection, 1849-1865 [early 1900s] to the Jackson County Historical Society Archives. This collection includes letters by Margaret Jane (Watts) Hays Overstreet, Colonel Upton Hays, and others. The John S. Watts, Sr. family moved from Kentucky to Van Buren (Cass Co.), Missouri, ca. 1839. His daughter, Margaret Jane Watts (1836-1923) married Upton Hays in 1852, and they lived on a farm near Westport, Jackson Co., Missouri. Upton Hays was a son of Boone Hays who bought the farm from his uncle, Morgan Boone, in the 1830's. The letters describe life in Jackson County in the mid-1800's and also contain stirring descriptions of the Civil War and Jayhawker raids in the area Colonel Upton Hays, 2nd (12th) Missouri Cavalry, Confederate States of America, was closely associated with William Clarke Quantrill. He was killed in a skirmish in 1862 and Margaret Hays was exiled from Jackson Co. by "Order No. 11" in 1863. Margaret Hays lived in Callaway Co., Missouri, until the end of the Civil War, then returned to Jackson County and lived there until 1872 when she migrated with her children to California where she homesteaded in Tulare Co. (later Kings Co.) in 1873, and married William Overstreet in 1877. The letters and transcripts are available online at wattshaysletters.com.

assailed Union patrols along the Missouri and Kansas border. In June 1862, they even successfully assaulted the Missouri River steamboat, *Little Blue*, at the landing at Sibley in Jackson County. The *Kansas City Journal* maintained that guerilla success was attributed to those who had remained pro-southern in sentiment, despite many of whom having previously taken the loyalty oath and given bond to the Union. It was maintained that guerillas were harbored and supported by those unfaithful to the Federal government. The *Journal* apparently overlooked or ignored the

Captain Jo Shelby

effects that Kansans, the loyalty oath, and the Governor's militia announcement had played on these recruitment efforts.

Throughout the spring and summer of 1862, significant recruiting efforts were taking place throughout all of western Missouri, and in particular Jackson County. Confederate officers including Colonel John T. Hughes, Colonel Gideon Thompson, Colonel John T. Coffee, Colonel J. Vard Cockrell, Colonel Sidney D. Jackman and Captain Joseph Orville "Jo" Shelby had joined the mission of Upton Hays and had entered the area determined to add recruits.

By August 1, Hughes and Thompson had joined Hays and Quantrill in Jackson County for the purpose of garnering recruitments into their ranks. They assembled near the Sni Mill and Blue Springs in eastern Jackson County at a farm owned by Francis R. Cowherd. Men soon poured onto the Cowherd Farm from the countryside and adjoining counties to answer the Southern call. Many lacked ammunition or proper military weapons. Those with ammunition were said to have possessed no more than two rounds. However, they reportedly rode well-trained horses and by August 10, their numbers had swelled to approximately 400 men. These men sorely needed proper military provisions and supplies to wage combat. This made the County Seat at Independence an attractive venue to attack.

17

BLOOD ON THE STREETS

The recruitment and guerilla activity in western Missouri was not ignored or overlooked by the Union military leadership in Missouri. Brigadier General John Schofield, having replaced General Halleck, issued an order on June 5 from his headquarters in St. Louis. Under his edict, the State of Missouri was divided into several military zones, known as the Districts of Missouri. Jackson County was placed in the Central District under the command of Brigadier General James Totten, stationed at Jefferson City. Immediately thereafter, the principal towns of Kansas City, Westport, and Independence in Jackson County were converted into Union military posts.

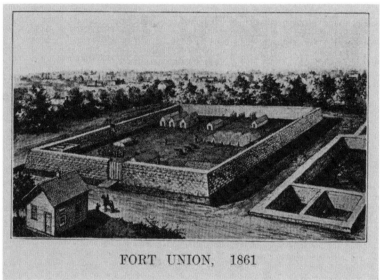

FORT UNION, 1861

In adherence to Schofield's directive, Lieutenant Colonel James T. Buel of the 7th Cavalry of the Missouri State Volunteers assumed command of the military post at Independence on June 7. He established his headquarters in the Southern Bank (later known as the McCoy Bank) located at 205 West Lexington Avenue, and a half-block west of the County Courthouse on the Square. Buel had under his command Companies B and D of the 7th Cavalry, in all approximately 350 men. The two-year-old Jackson County Jail became headquarters of the provost marshal, an office similar to that of the military police and a position with unmolested and dictatorial authority. Lieutenant Charles W. Meryhew, with approximately 26 men assigned to him, was named the post's Provost Marshal.

Buel then stationed his main force on the Lexington-Westport Road (today, roughly U.S. 24 Highway) in a field owned by Samuel Woodson, attorney and former Congressman from Independence, and located about one mile southwest of Buel's headquarters. Woodson had constructed on his land a rock wall some half-mile southwest of Buel's headquarters. The wall served as a fence that extended west from the end of Railroad-Cut eastward about one-half mile. The troops positioned on these grounds were under the direct authority of Captain Breckenridge.

Over the next two months, Buel on several occasions dispatched Breckenridge and Captain Aaron Thomas of the Missouri Enrolled Militia on various expeditions to scour the woods and ravines for guerillas and their recruiting efforts. While they did discover some rebel activity, they reportedly found nothing that would warrant any concerns that an attack upon Independence was eminent, or even likely.

The findings and conclusions of Breckenridge, Thomas and others assigned by Buel to the task of searching for guerilla activity were inconsistent with other reports being released throughout the region. On August 8, Colonel E. C. Catherwood, 6th Missouri Cavalry, in Sedalia, Pettis County, Missouri, sent a communication to the Adjutant General of Missouri that there were over 500 armed guerilla forces in eastern Jackson County. Newspapers including the *Liberty Tribune* in Clay County and the *Kansas City Daily Journal of Commerce* in Kansas City wrote articles about the increased size of Confederate and guerrilla troops in the region. Some reports even estimated that there were over 1,200 rebels forming in the woods.

As early as Sunday, August 3, the *Daily Journal* warned that an attack by Bushwhackers could be expected anytime and that loyal men needed to

Captain William Clarke Quantrill

organize immediately in defense of the anticipated assault on Independence. Six days later, the *Daily Journal* proclaimed reliable sources had reported that approximately 800 men under Quantrill[6] and Hays were threatening Independence.

While these editorial opinions, newspaper accounts, and military reports expressed dire warnings, Buel chose to ignore or disregard these threats, or the serious potential of an impending attack upon his military post. To Buel, the military reports, accounts and stories of rebel recruitment with their eyes on Independence were nothing more than groundless and baseless rumors, and he had grown tired of such untruths. Buel was convinced that he had his military post well under his command and control.

---

[6] During the Border War years between Missouri and Kansas in the mid- to late-1850s, William Clarke Quantrill had gone by the name of Charlie Hart. According to Quantrill guerilla, William H. Gregg, of Jackson County, Quantrill's men referred to him during the Civil War by the name of "Charlie."

CHAPTER III

Making Preparations to Attack Independence

Notables Engaged at the First Battle of Independence
Confederate   Union

Confederate	Union
Boyd, Lieutenant Colonel John R.*	Axline, Jacob (Captain)
Brown, [--?--] (Captain)*	Breckenridge, [--?--] (Captain)
	Buel, James T. (Lieutenant
Chambers, B (Captain)*	Colonel)
Chiles, Christopher "Kit"*	Burris, John T. (Colonel)
Clark, Sam (Captain)*	Cochran, [--?--] (Captain)
Cockrell, J. Vard (Colonel)	Herington, [--?--] (Lieutenant)
Coffee, John T. (Colonel)	Jewett, Homer (Private)
	Meryhew, Charles W.
Gregg, William H. (Lieutenant)	(Lieutenant; Provost Marshal)
Hart, John R. (Major)*	Rodewald, [--?--] (Captain)
	Thomas, Aaron (Reverend)
Hays, Upton (Colonel)	(Captain)
Hughes, John T. (Colonel)*	
Jackman, Sidney D. (Colonel)	
Price, Sterling (General)	
McCorkle, John Gregg (Lieutenant)	
Quantrill, William Clarke (Captain)	
Shelby, Joseph Orville "Jo" (Captain)	
Thompson, Gideon (Colonel)	
Todd, George (Lieutenant)	
Wortle, [--?--] (Major)*	
Younger, Thomas Coleman "Cole"	

* = killed in action

While Lieutenant Colonel Buel may have disbelieved reports of an impending attack, he did recognize the benefit of reinforcements. During the first week of August, Buel sent out a request to Lexington and to Colonel John T. Burris stationed at Fort Leavenworth seeking additional troops to defend the county seat. When Burris received the missive from Buel, he was in Kansas City and in response Burris quickly dispatched troops to Independence. Burris ordered Captain Jacob Axline, Company B,

21

2nd Battery Cavalry, Missouri State Militia, and his company stationed at Westport, to immediately report to Independence.

In compliance to Burris' directive, Axline, with approximately 50 men, arrived in Independence in the late night hours of Sunday, August 10. Axline then had his company encamped in the southwest section of Independence, near the Railroad-Cut on the Independence-Westport Road, and next to the troops under Breckenridge. Unlike Breckenridge's men, Axline and his militia did not have benefit of tents. They were compelled to retire on the grounds with nothing more than blanket roles. With the arrival of Axline and his troops from Westport, Buel now had the Missouri Militia and Missouri Volunteers under his command with a total force of about 500 men.[7]

Many of Quantrill's men and other recent recruits were well-familiar with the layout of the town of Independence. Some probably had even been inside the town to sign the unpopular loyalty oath to the Union; but, afterwards, had darted off into the woods to volunteer their support to the rebellion. Of all the various accounts relating to the rebels' knowledge about the layout of the town of Independence, the story of **Thomas Coleman "Cole" Younger** and his reconnoitering efforts within Independence is the most unique and alluring.

On August 10, Hays reportedly dispatched Cole Younger, a recent recruit, to Independence to scout the town. Younger rode into town in a buggy dressed as a woman. He then proceeded to hand out apples or doughnuts to town folks while he spied on the environs of the town. As the disguised young man began to leave Independence, a Federal sentry demanded identification. In response to this request, Younger pulled out his revolver and promptly shot and killed the soldier. Younger thereafter rapidly fled and escaped.[8]

---

[7] The distinction between members of the militia and the volunteers was that the militia only had jurisdiction to protect the Union within the State of Missouri while the volunteers had authority to put down the rebellion inside and outside the state.

[8] Younger later verified the story in his own narrative written some 40 years

While the Younger story may be nothing more than legend, there is no question that the young man had personal reasons to have felt revenge in his heart. His father, **Henry Washington Younger**, who had been Jackson County Court judge for 8 years and twice elected to the Missouri Legislature, had been murdered on the Harrisonville-Independence Road on June 20, 1862. At the time of his death, Henry Younger was the United States Mail postal contractor of Harrisonville, and he was in route to Independence for a delivery. His death was reported to have been at the hands of Kansas troops, who it is said, took his watch and diamond stud; but, failed to take about $3,200 that was purportedly contained in his money belt. From that moment on, his son, Cole, became a willing Confederate recruit bent on killing Federal troops.

Reconnoitering efforts and accounts aside, Buel continued to receive reports of guerilla activities in the day or two leading up to the attack on Independence. Local newspapers continued writing their stories of such activity, and during the weekend of August 9, Mrs. Lucinda Wilson of the Blue Springs/Sni-A-Bar area (about 10 miles east of Independence) traveled to the County Seat to meet with Buel. Mrs. Wilson's purpose in meeting with Buel at his office on the first floor of the Southern Bank was to warn him of an impending attack by guerilla and Confederate troops. Present also at this meeting were both Captain Rodewald, a baker and former city councilman of Independence, and Captain Aaron Thomas, Company E of the Missouri Enrolled State Militia, and former minister of the North Methodist Church in Independence. Mrs. Wilson also told Buel and the two officers that she had seen as many as 1,000 to 1,200 men near the Blue Springs. Buel failed to heed her warnings and summarily dismissed her after their interview.

---

after the War. However, he also verified other mythical tales as well. See, Younger, Coleman. *The Story of Cole Younger, By Himself.* Originally published in 1903. (Springfield, Mo.: Oak Hills Publishing, 1996).

Mrs. Wilson was incensed over Buel's rebuke, and she went forthwith to the residence of **General Samuel D. Lucas**. Lucas had been a long-time resident of Independence; he had taken the loyalty oath to the Federal and State provisional governments; he had served as a general in the Missouri State Militia during the 1830's where he had participated in the military actions against the Mormons. Lucas, after hearing Mrs. Wilson's account, went immediately to see Buel at his headquarters. Lucas informed Buel that he truly believed that Mrs. Wilson had related factual information to him. He further admonished Buel to consider Wilson's remarks as trustworthy and credible. Apparently, Buel was growing anxious about these stories. He reminded Lucas that he had recently sent Breckenridge out on an 11-day scout and that he had found no signs of an organized enemy force. Lucas left the meeting without having made any more headway than had Mrs. Wilson.

Despite the repeated warnings of recruitment and large numbers of guerilla and Confederate activity in Jackson County, Buel took no formal action to fortify or prepare a defense against an attack. His failure to act would ultimately be his downfall, as in the end, the reports and stories proved to be true.

CHAPTER IV

Blood Battle in Independence

Around 4 a.m. on August 11, 1862, some 750 Confederate and guerilla troops under the command of **Colonel John T. Hughes** rode into Independence. When the men assembled in town, they dismounted and left their horses corralled around the Courthouse Square. Hughes had entered the town by the Big Spring Road (today, Spring Branch Road), and divided his men into two columns.

One column was given two directives: 1) to attack the provost guard

stationed at the Jackson County Jail, and 2) to seize the Southern Bank building occupied by Colonel Buel. The main body under Hughes was then divided into two groups. They were to advance from east to west along two parallel roads with the assigned mission to advance upon the Union encampment in the southwestern edge of town. The entire Union force was asleep and wholly unprepared for the attack.

From the Courthouse Square, Quantrill led his troops west down Lexington Avenue towards Buel's headquarters and north on Main Street towards the Jackson County Jail. Forces under Hughes followed behind Quantrill's guerillas; but, they continued their march west on Lexington Avenue and Walnut Street, and then proceeded south on Pleasant Street to wage their assault against the Union encampment. Overall there were three principal hotspots of action on or around the Square and streets of Independence that morning.

Assault on Union Encampment

Once Hughes had passed behind Quantrill's guerillas near Buel's headquarters, he and his men continued westward on Lexington and Walnut aiming to seize the Union troops in their encampment in the southwest section of town. The Union forces were weary eyed and still asleep when the initial Confederate attack was made. The Federals were promptly exposed to a steady fire from the advancing rebels who were well concealed in the front and rear of the Union troops. As Hughes led his men into the Federal camp, he was shot and instantly fell dead. His subordinate, **Colonel Gideon Thompson**, took over command of the Confederate troops and he continued his forward advance upon the Union camp.

The men under the combined commands of Breckenridge and Axline were completely caught off guard by the rebel advance. To protect his men from the Confederate gunfire, Axline moved his men down to Woodson's rock fence located at the southwest corner of the campground. At that spot, the wall crossed a gutter from three to four feet deep and Axline posted his men at that location. Lieutenant Herington, of Company E, Missouri State Militia, came to the assistance of Axline. From this position, Axline and Herington were able to protect their front and flanks. The location behind the barrier also enabled the Federal forces to cover three-fourths of the camp with their musket fire. The refuge

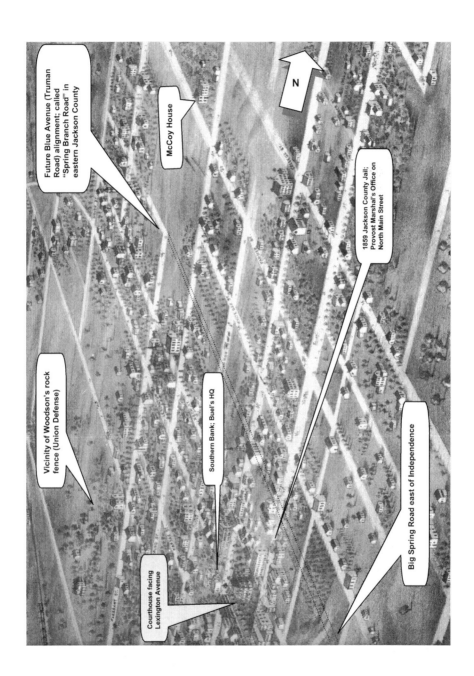

behind the barricade allowed Axline and Herington's men to make a valiant defense of their encampment as it proved to be a formidable defensive position to the oncoming charge of the enemy force.

Not long after the Union troops had secured their strong defensive position behind the rock fence, Breckenridge, 7th Missouri Volunteer Cavalry, and senior officer in the camp, attempted to surrender the Federal soldiers. Whether out of fear or something else, Breckenridge tore a piece of his white shirt and hoisted it upon the rock fence. Spotting the symbol of surrender, Herington followed by Axline, promptly proceeded about 400 yards west where they met Breckenridge, who, by then, held a white cloth tied to a gun-stick. It was Breckenridge's intention to hoist the surrender flag. As he began to do so, Axline countermanded the order. There are reports that some of Axline's men wrestled the white flag from Breckenridge.

Axline took command of the Union troops after Breckenridge's failed attempt to conclude the engagement. For about the next four hours, Confederate forces made four to five unsuccessful assaults against the Union troops who were well-protected by the rock wall. Each time the Union militia and volunteers were able to thwart these attacks by inflicting significant casualties upon the Confederates. Both Thompson and Hays suffered wounds during these failed attempts to capture the wall.

Although many Union troops remained to fight over the wall, some had fled the encampment after the initial assaults. Private Homer Jewett and several other members of the militia were among those who had sought refuge in or about the residence of William and Eleanor (Waddle) McCoy on Farmer Street, a few blocks northwest of the County Courthouse on the Square.[9]

---

[9]William McCoy had been elected in 1849 as the first Mayor of Independence. The McCoy home remains today as a private residence at 410 West Farmer, Independence, Missouri, and is a recognized historic site with relevance to the Santa Fe, California, and Oregon National Historic Trail system.

There they once again found themselves engaged in combat with their adversaries. This time they were confronted principally by Quantrill's guerillas. According to John McCorkle, one of Quantrill's raiders, the Union troops inside and around the **McCoy residence** were unable to cause them any harm. In the end, Jewett and his fellow soldiers abandoned the McCoy property and grounds to the guerillas and successfully made their escape to Kansas City some ten miles to the west.

Taking the Provost Marshal's Headquarters

Another key location during the early morning attack was the Provost Marshal's headquarters in the Jackson County Jail on Main Street (one block north of the Jackson County Courthouse). According to John McCorkle's report of the incident, Lieutenant William H. Gregg, a guerilla under Quantrill, dispatched about 10 men under Lieutnant George Todd to seize the Jail. Like the Union troops sleeping in the encampment southwest of town, the bulk of the provost guard, too, was sleeping in their camp just north of the Jail. After leading his small force north on Main Street, Todd successfully assaulted the Jail. Provost Marshal Captain Meryhew and his guard did not stay and fight like their comrades struggling behind the rock fence. Whether the provost guard was able to fire off a round at the advancing guerillas is speculative. It is unquestioned, however, that Meryhew and his men fled from the attack to safety in Kansas City.

After Todd's men had successfully dispensed with the provost and his guard, they entered the provost marshal's office and seized the Jackson County Jail. They sledge hammered the locks of the jail cells imprisoning several male and female inmates. One prisoner was Jim Knowles, the elected City Marshal of Independence. Earlier in the month, he had piloted Captain Aaron Thomas, acting under orders of Buel, to hunt down Bushwhackers. Knowles had led Thomas and his troops into the Blue Cut neighborhood of eastern Jackson County where they surprised guerrillas George Todd, Ed Koger, and John Little. Todd escaped; but, Koger and Little were killed. Shortly, thereafter, and in an unrelated incident, Knowles killed an old Irishman who was drunk and *"cutting up."* Despite being the City Marshal, the Provost Marshal had Knowles arrested for the murder. Knowles was behind bars at the time Todd and his entourage broke the pad locks on the metal doors of the jail cells.

The rebels also found incarcerated inside the **1859 Jail,** three purported southern prisoners: Bill Bassham, Frank Harbaugh and James Noel, each with suspect secessionist backgrounds. Bassham had been a stage driver on the old Santa Fe Trail working for the government; but, he had quit and returned to his home in Independence about the time Jim Knowles had killed the Irishman. It was said that Bassham was not connected with the War in any way; but, someone preferred the charge against him that he was a Quantrill raider. This allegation had led to his incarceration.

Frank Harbaugh was a local farmer, who like Bassham,

was suspected of being a rebel sympathizer. Bassham and Harbaugh were both scheduled to be executed by a firing squad the following day. Todd had both men released from jail.

After Todd released these two men, Bassham insisted on being given a shotgun to kill the men who had incarcerated him. Harbaugh reportedly ran out of the jail and, according to McCorkle, was never seen again.

The guerillas also released James Noel, who was the owner of a mill near Lone Jack, in southeastern Jackson County. Noel, too, was being held on suspicion of having consorted with rebels in the woods near the Sni-A-Bar. There was little question what plans Todd had for Knowles. Out of revenge for Knowles' involvement in the killings of Koger and Little earlier that month, Todd shot and killed Knowles inside his jail cell.

Assault on Lt. Col. Buel's Headquarters

The third area of attack contemporaneously made at the time of the assault on the Union Camp and provost marshal's office and the Jackson County Jail was against Buel's headquarters in the **Southern Bank building.**

Buel not only had troops inside the bank, but there were 21 men, 16 of whom were Missouri Volunteers under Rodewald, stationed at the armory on Lexington Avenue directly across the street north of Buel's headquarters.

When the guerillas made their initial charge upon Buel, the rebels were caught in a cross fire, and the infamous guerilla, Christopher "Kit" Chiles, was mortally wounded. The

siege of the building proved to be long and complex. Despite several attempts, guerillas had been unsuccessful in gaining control of Buel's command post. Union troops on both sides of the street fired at every rebel attempt to capture the bank.

There are accounts of heroics on both sides in defending and attacking. In the end, a strategy was developed to conclude the siege. According to Cole Younger, Hays asked for volunteers to burn a building adjacent to the bank building. Younger and others gathered wood chips and made a fire in a livery stable directly to the south of the Southern Bank. As the fire began to rise, smoke enveloped the bank building and encircled the street. The fighting continued for some time before Buel realized the seriousness of the situation. He raised a white flag; but, he was insistent that he would only surrender to Thompson and not to Quantrill. Buel wanted to ensure that he and his men surrendered to the Confederate forces and not to Quantrill and his guerilla warriors, to guarantee that his men would be treated humanely and as prisoners of war. He feared Quantrill's treatment would be inhumane if he and his troops were taken into custody by the guerilla chief.

Throughout the siege at the bank, Axline and his forces remained well defended behind the rock barricade. Every charge made by Confederate troops had been repulsed. It was not until Axline received word of Buel's surrender that he gave up the fight, and ordered his men to lay down their arms. His remaining troops—at least those not dead, mortally wounded or fleeing westward to Kansas City—were then marched from their encampment to Buel's command post outside the bank building.

The Blood Totals of the First Battle of Independence

The combined guerilla and Confederate attack on Independence had been a complete debacle to the Federal government and most specifically for Buel himself. He had failed to heed all of the warnings and notifications that he had received of an impending attack. In the end, this compelled him to capitulate.

After terms were negotiated, Buel and his remaining force surrendered to the seriously wounded Thompson outside the Southern Bank building.

Buel had lost his entire military post, and he and his men had become prisoners of war.

As the surrender terms were being negotiated, guerillas went in search of Captain Thomas. They located Thomas inside his family residence about a mile from camp, where he was promptly seized. Unlike the treatment afforded the other Union troops, Thomas was not as fortunate. After his capture by members of Quantrill's guerillas, Thomas was summarily executed. His murder, like that of Knowles, was in retaliation for his alleged involvement in the earlier killings of Ed Koger and John Little. George Todd became angry over the shooting of Thomas because he had not been afforded the opportunity to personally have the honor of slaying Thomas himself.[10]

With the exception of the murders of Knowles and Thomas, it was reported that the Confederates and guerillas behaved themselves very orderly. Axline expressed his personal acknowledgments on how the Union troops were treated by the enemy after the battle.

Following their victory, Confederate and guerilla troops seized and took control of the vanquished quartermaster and commissary stores where they obtained much needed contraband, property and munitions. Their bounty was enough to fill about 20 wagonloads. Once they secured their supplies and spent time tending to their dead and wounded, Thompson had the Union troops paroled.[11] Thereafter, Thompson ordered the evacuation of

---

[10] Reverend Aaron Thomas is buried in Woodlawn Cemetery, Independence, Missouri. His tombstone reads: "Several years a member of the Missouri Conference of the M.E. Church, was elected Captain of Company E, 2nd Battalion, M.S.M. [Missouri State Militia]. Killed in the Battle of Independence, August 11, 1862. Aged 46 years, 11 months."

[11] During the Civil War, soldiers who were paroled during or after a battle were required to give their solemn word and oath that they would not engage in battle against those who had granted them parole until such time as the paroled soldiers were properly exchanged for a prisoner or prisoners held by their own army. Meaning that once Buel's men were paroled they were not allowed to fight until they were exchanged (paroled) for Confederate prisoners. On December 3, 1861, General Halleck wrote from his office in St. Louis that prisoners ought to be exchanged, as it was simply a convention, and the fact that they had been exchanged would not prevent their being tried for treason, if

the town. It was late in the afternoon, around 4:00 p.m., when the victorious rebel forces abandoned Independence.

As the victors withdrew from the vanquished county seat, they traveled southeast in the general direction of the Blue Springs. When they were a few miles east of Independence, Quantrill and his guerrillas broke off from the main column of Confederates now under the command of Hays.[12] Quantrill took his men to the Morgan Walker farm for much needed rest and seclusion.[13] Hays had assumed the position as the Confederate commanding officer because of the death of Hughes and the serious shoulder injury in which

desired, after the war. With some exceptions, the parole and exchange of prisoners by both Union and Confederate Army's continued until General Ulysses S. Grant discontinued the practice by order dated April 17, 1864.

[12] Colonel Upton Hays was born on March 29, 1832, in Callaway County, Missouri; but, he grew-up in Jackson County. His father was Boone Hays, a grandson of Daniel Boone, the famous trailblazer and pioneer. His father, Boone Hays, settled his family in Westport, Jackson County, Missouri in 1837. Boone Hays died in California in 1850. Within a few weeks after the Battle of Lone Jack, Colonel Upton Hays would be killed in a skirmish near Newtonia, Missouri when he met his death leading a charge against Federal troops from Wisconsin. He is buried in Forest Hill Cemetery, Kansas City, Missouri.

[13] Morgan Walker and his sons had been pro-southern slaveholders in eastern Jackson County before the Civil War. In December 1860, Quantrill, then known as Charlie Hart, had led Kansas free-state men into an ambush on the Walker farm. The Kansans had planned on seizing and stealing Walker's slaves and other property and return them to Kansas. Quantrill, knowing of their plans, turned on his Kansas acquaintances and plotted with the Walkers to kill the Kansans. Three of the five men were killed, and the other two escaped despite suffering serious wounds. The actions taken that night by Quantrill endeared him to Morgan Walker, his family and neighbors. From that evening on, an integral part of the legend of William Clarke Quantrill (no longer Charlie Hart) had been born.

Thompson had suffered during the assault of the Federal encampment. Hays led his troops southeast towards Lone Jack to encamp for the night.

The casualty totals for the Battle of Independence were assessed as follows: Union: killed 26; wounded, 30; and about 150 captured. The combined Confederate and guerillas casualties was about 32 killed and 40 wounded. Among their officers killed, in addition to Hughes and "Kit" Chiles, were Lieutenant Colonel John R. Boyd; Major John R. Hart; Major Wortle; Captain Brown; Captain Sam Clark; and, Captain B. Chambers. It took days before all of the wounded were removed to Kansas City, or the dead were buried.

Independence had been waylaid. Buel had to point the blame for the loss on others. He had Breckenridge arrested after he received Axline's account of Breckenridge's cowardly conduct and his attempted surrender at the rock wall. He also brought charges against Captain Cochran who had reportedly hid in a cellar throughout the battle.

Ironically, these two militia officers were not deemed to be the only weak leaks in the military defense of the post at Independence. Buel, too, was brought up on charges for dereliction of duty and failure to properly prepare for an attack that he should have anticipated and expected.

The paroled Federal soldiers remained in Independence for a few days before they marched to Kansas City, and then traveled on to Fort Leavenworth to be exchanged for Confederate prisoners. After their exchange, Buel and his troops were transferred to Benton Barracks in St. Louis. Instead of being prosecuted, Buel and his two co-defendants, Breckenridge and Cochran, were mustered out of the Army.

The combined Confederate and guerilla capture of Independence was a complete disaster for the Union. Federal commanders became fearful that other raids would be made against other military posts in western Missouri, including Lexington, Westport and Kansas City. Soon, rumors were buzzing across the wire that Confederates were in route to Lexington. These stories proved untrue.

BLOOD ON THE STREETS

The reports that as many as 4,000 to 5,000 southern forces were massing in the Lone Jack area of southeastern Jackson County were, however, determined to be legitimate. The reported estimates as to the number of Confederates troops were significantly higher than the actual numbers; but, such inflated accounts helped fuel the fire of fear and the cry for Union reinforcements.

CHAPTER V

On the Road to Lone Jack

Notables Engaged at the Battle of Lone Jack
Confederate   Union

Confederate	Union
Cockrell, J. Vard (Reverend) (Colonel)	Brawner, H. M. (Captain)
Coffee, John T. (Colonel)	Develin, James C. (Lieutenant)
Gregg, William H. (Lieutenant)	Foster, Emery S. (Major)
Hays, Upton (Colonel)	Foster, Melville (Captain)*
Hunter, Dewitt C. (Colonel)	Ransom, Wyllis C. (Major)
Jackman, Sidney D. (Colonel)	Scott, James M. (Sergeant)
Noel, James	
Poindexter, [--?--] (Colonel)	
Rains, James S. (General)	
Tracy, John (Colonel)	
Winfrey, Caleb (Doctor; Captain, promoted to Major)	
Younger, Thomas Coleman "Cole"	

* = killed in action

The road to Lone Jack began with Confederate recruitment in western Missouri following their defeat at Pea Ridge, continued through the capture of Independence and climaxed with a Confederate victory at the Battle of Lone Jack on August 16, 1862.

The report of the rebel success at Lone Jack was succinctly summarized in a report sent to General James G. Blunt, commander of the Department of Kansas, from Major Wyllis C. Ransom of the 6th Kansas Cavalry the day after the engagement: *"United States troops were surprised yesterday morning by the rebel forces of Colonels Coffee and Cockrell . . . and after a heavy resistance they were obliged to surrender with great loss. Our troops had a battery of two pieces, which is now in possession of the enemy."*[14]

Following the victory at Independence, Colonel Upton

---

[14] O.R. series 1, Vol. XIII, Part 1, pp. 236.

Hays, now in command of the Confederate troops that had been engaged at Independence, led his men southeast and encamped at the Harbaugh farm some 12-miles northwest of Lone Jack.[15] Hays would soon be joined by other Confederate troops. Captain William Clarke Quantrill and his guerillas remained at the Morgan Walker farm in eastern Jackson County near Blue Springs.

General James S. Rains assigned Colonel Vard Cockrell the duty to venture into western Missouri to further the recruiting efforts previously commenced by the late Colonel John T. Hughes, Colonel Thompson and Colonel Hays. Around the first of August, Colonels Sidney D. Jackman and Dewitt C. Hunter and Captain Jo Shelby had joined Colonel Cockrell and his unit. They had all departed Arkansas on the same assigned mission. As they traveled north through Missouri, their ranks began to swell. In Butler County, Cockrell united his men with those who had been recruited by Colonel John T. Coffee, formerly of the Missouri State Guard, and Colonel John Tracy of the Confederate Army.

By the night of August 14, Cockrell and his men had reached Johnson County. That evening, Cockrell turned his command over to Hunter as Cockrell desired to visit his family, who were still living at the time in the County Seat at Warrensburg. Shelby and his men did not go into camp with the other Confederate troops. Instead, he and his men continued on to Lafayette County to recruit troops in or around Shelby's home at Waverly.

On the morning of August 15, the Confederate forces under Cockrell, Hunter, Tracy, Coffee, and Jackman, numbering about 1,200 men, began a northwesterly march towards Jackson County and the hamlet of Lone Jack. After the day-long march, Hunter's forces encamped about two miles southwest of the town. Likewise, Coffee and Tracy, who were independent of Hunter, rested their troops that evening as well.

---

[15] At the time of this writing, it is unknown if this may be James Harbaugh whom Todd had released from the Jackson County Jail a week prior, or a relative. In the 1860 U.S. Census for Big Cedar (today, Lee's Summit), Blue Township, Jackson County, Missouri, enumerated is Franklin Harbaugh, age 29, with his family, Mary E., 22; George W., 5; Amanda, 3; and, Minnie, 1. James Harbaugh was not located in the 1860 Jackson County census.

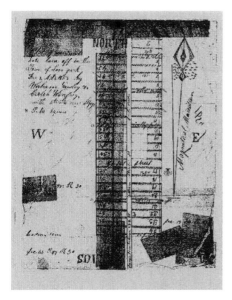

1853 plat for Easley and Winfrey's Addition, which became the site of the 1862 Battle of Lone Jack

The men under Coffee camped at the Graham farm about a half mile southwest of Lone Jack, while Tracy's men stopped at the David Arnold farm about two miles south of the town. Hays and his men had traveled south from Independence and were also in the vicinity. Before reaching his home in Warrensburg, Cockrell heard reports that Union forces were advancing toward Lone Jack. Rather than surprising his family with a visit, he immediately returned to the camp that his subordinate, Colonel Hunter, had established.

Not unlike their Confederate counterparts, Union troops had been on the move since the capture of Independence. On August 14, Major Emery S. Foster and his troops under orders issued by General Totten in Jefferson City led his mounted forces on a rapid march from Warrensburg to Lexington.[16] Initial reports after the fall of Independence were that Confederate and Quantrill guerillas intended to attack the County Seat of Lafayette County.

Totten immediately countermanded his prior orders when it was discovered that the rebel forces were not advancing towards

---

[16] Major Foster was a native of Missouri. In fact, he and Confederate Col. Cockrell were living in Warrensburg, Johnson County, Missouri at the outbreak of the War and their families were still living in Warrensburg at the time of the Battle of Lone Jack. Foster lived until December 23, 1902. He died in Oakland, California at the age of 64. It is reported that he had traveled to California about two months before he passed away. He had had hoped that the weather on the west coast would help him recover from the wounds he had suffered at the Battle of Lone Jack. Foster's wife Jessie (Beall), formerly of Granby, Missouri, and his daughter Ms. Jessie Foster, survived his death.

Lexington; but, were instead traveling towards Lone Jack. Receiving a telegraph directive from Totten, Foster redirected his cavalry to seize the town of Lone Jack. The overall Union plan was for Foster to hold the town until he was reinforced. Totten had also dispatched Colonel Fitz Henry Warren and his Iowa troops stationed in Clinton, Henry County, to join Foster. From the west, Blunt's men stationed at Fort Scott, Kansas, were to reinforce Foster as well. It was further reported that other Union forces under Colonel Burris and Major Ransom were in route from the Missouri-Kansas border.

Around 9 p.m. on August 15, Foster and his force estimated to be some 800 strong, reached Lone Jack. His army was comprised of detachments from five companies of the 7th Cavalry, Missouri Volunteers; three companies of the 6th Cavalry, Missouri State Militia; two companies of the 8th Cavalry, Missouri State Militia, and three companies of the 2nd Battalion of Cavalry, Missouri State Militia, together with a section of two pieces of the 3rd Indiana Battery. Foster placed his two cannons at the southern edge of the road at the entrance to the town. He next had the colors posted above the Cave House, a tavern owned by Mr. and Mrs. Bart B. and Lucinda Cave, where he established his headquarters. The beleaguered troops rested in the streets of the village. They had been in their saddles about 30 straight hours and were fatigued.

The town of Lone Jack was a crossroads village located on a summit of a high prairie ridge overlooking the surrounding country. Only one tree stood in the town—an old jack oak tree, which gave city fathers' the inspiration for its name.

With a population of around 2,000, it was situated in the southeastern corner of Jackson County. Bisecting the town running north and south was the Harrisonville-Independence Road (today, Bynum Road), a highway that connected the County Seats of Cass to the south and Jackson to the north. On each side of the road, there were dwelling houses, shops and stores. Behind the structures to the east and west were cultivated fields surrounded by native Osage Orange trees, or hedge rows.

Union troops occupied this section of the town, known as New Town, which was to the south of the older section of town.

Situated in the "New Town" were the spacious Cave House, a blacksmith shop, and other businesses.

Despite the proximity of the opposing forces gathered in or around Lone Jack, neither side was fully aware of the presence of the other. For precautionary reasons, Foster, after he had made camp in the town, dispatched some troops to scout the perimeter of the area.

BLOOD ON THE STREETS

CHAPTER VI

Blood Splattering in Lone Jack

The Late Evening Hours of August 15, 1862

Union Camp

After Major Foster had positioned his men in and around Lone Jack, he ordered his brother, Captain Melville Foster, to direct all the commissioned officers to gather for a meeting to consider their options and develop a strategy.[17] During the conference, Major Foster informed his officers that earlier that day he had received a report that a small party of Colonel Nugent's battalion had gathered intelligence of having located Colonel Coffee's rebel forces just to the immediate south of Lone Jack. This led to a debate on the merits of launching a surprise night attack upon the Confederate troops that evening.

During the staff meeting, it was learned that the officer in command of the Indiana Battery, Lieutenant James C. Develin, had forgotten to supply the two cannons with proper ammunition. Rather than *canister shot*, which dispersed like a shotgun and was devastating to troops, they only had *round shot*—traditional cannon balls—in their arsenal. Major Foster was incensed by this breach of military safety and protocol. It would not be the last time that Foster would lose patience with Develin. Foster had a strong hatred and antagonism towards secessionists. This was because Confederates had previously killed one of his brothers earlier in the War. He was also well noted for his aggressiveness against rebel troops. For these reasons alone, Foster was determined to launch an immediate assault to disperse the enemy. His officers concurred, and the decision was made to proceed with the night

---

[17] Matthews, Matt, and Kip Lindberg. "Shot All to Pieces: The Battle of Lone Jack, Missouri, 1862." *North and South* (January 2004): 7:1, 70. Foster is identified as "Morris" in Eakin, Joanne Chiles. *Battle of Lone Jack.* (Independence, Mo.: Two Trails Publishing, 2001).

attack. It was near 10 p.m. on a very hot and humid August night with temperatures in the low 90's and rain in the forecast when Foster's men set out in search of a battle.

When the Union advance guard left camp, they initially encountered a local farmer who mistook them for Confederate troops under Colonel Poindexter. He mistakenly informed the Federal soldiers that he could direct them to the two Confederate forces under Coffee and Tracy. According to the farmer, the Confederates were encamped in a meadow just south of Lone Jack and east of the Harrisonville-Independence Road, which was, at that time, a lane between split rail fences.

Armed with this information, Major Foster directed a scouting party to capture the Confederate pickets, and he ordered the cannons forward. To muffle the sound of the two cannons, the wheels were covered with blankets, and then pulled down the lane. The Confederate pickets were reportedly captured without the firing of any shots. Tracy and Coffee's men, however, were soon to be overwhelmed.

The artillery was brought into position, commanding the lane through which the troops had passed. Skirmishers were thrown out on each flank and to the front, and the whole column moved forward. After advancing about three-fourths of a mile, between the town and the camp of the rebels, the Confederate cavalry charged down the lane and into the Union troops. They were soon repulsed by a volley of musketry, and they scattered in all directions.

The Union cannon fire soon lit-up the night sky as the rebel camps were shelled by the battery with good effect. Coffee's men soon quickly retreated and fled into the night. Likewise, Tracy's men scrambled, seeking shelter in the woods.

With the enemy having been overrun and dispersed into the countryside, and with no further demonstrations on their part being anticipated, the Union command returned to Lone Jack, arriving at around 11 p.m. Many of the wounded from the night assault were taken back to the Cave House to receive medical care and treatment. Major Foster then ordered a yellow flag to be draped on the façade of the Cave House to symbolize its status as a hospital.

Although the night attack had successfully disrupted and

disbursed the two Confederate encampments, it had certain unintended negative consequences. Some members of the Union Cavalry became confused in the darkness of the night and shot into the Indiana Battery believing them to be Confederate troops. Four members of the battery were killed by friendly fire. Furthermore, Major Foster became convinced that Develin was inebriated during the night assault. Develin was placed under arrest, and the artillery command was turned over to Sergeant James M. Scott.

Finally, the night assault only helped to unite the surrounding Confederate troops as the cannon and musket fire not only awakened them from sleep; but, it had provided notice that Federal troops were within close proximity.

In the end, this proved the largest downfall. It had given the spread-out Confederates time to coalesce and gather their command and prepare for a counter attack the following morning.

Later in defending his action, Major Foster explained that he would neither have discharged his cannons nor made any night attack if he had known that Colonel Warren and his Iowans were not in the vicinity. He asserted that his scouts had, in fact, made contact with Warren, and for that reason he felt that reinforcements were at hand.

They were not!

The remainder of the night Union troops slept in the streets of Lone Jack under arms, while Major Foster and his staff slumbered inside the Cave House, while the wounded and lame from the night's engagement received medical attention.

The Early Morning Hours of August 16, 1862

Confederate Camps

In the early morning hours of August 16, the Confederate commanders gathered to discuss a strategy for later daybreak. Tracy had been able to reassemble his men in the darkness following the unexpected attack by the Union troops. As to Coffee and his men, there was no word as to their whereabouts. The two commands had gotten completely separated in the confusion of the night. Tracy after regaining control of his troops broke camp and moved his force to Hunter, where Cockrell had resumed command. Cockrell then dispatched two swift horsemen to locate Hays and ordered his troops to advance.

Around midnight, word reached Hays that Federal forces were inside Lone Jack. Hays awakened his men and ordered them to mount in order to join up with Cockrell and the other Confederate troops. When Hays arrived at the Kreeger farm, Tracy and Cockrell were awaiting him on their horses alongside the road. An order was sent to Hunter to bring up the remainder of his men and to unit at a nearby farmstead. The combined forces then advanced to the mill owned by James Noel.[18] After the men were assembled, Cockrell held a council of war. Present were Jackman, Hunter, Tracy and Hays. They agreed that they lacked sufficient

---

[18] This was the same James Noel who had been released from the Jackson County Jail by George Todd only five days earlier, after Todd and his guerrillas had seized the Jail during the raid on Independence. Union speculations of his secessionist views had been correct. During the Battle of Lone Jack, James Noel was a member of Captain Winfrey's Company under Col. Hunter. Dr. Caleb Winfrey had been a long-time resident of Lone Jack and had served in the Mexican War under Col. Alexander Doniphan of Clay County, Missouri.

information as to the size of the opposing force. They were also admittedly concerned to go into battle without benefit of Coffee's troops. In the end, the conclusion was made to launch a clandestine early morning attack upon the Union forces gathered at Lone Jack.

The Confederate battle plan was for the troops under Hunter, Jackman and Tracy to advance mounted to the western outskirts of Lone Jack. There the Confederates would dismount and form into three columns and stealthily advance upon the Union army at daybreak. The attack would be made from west to east with Hunter's men composing the right flank, Tracy's troops marking the left flank, and Jackman in the center.

The strategy further called for Hays and his mounted troops to feint an attack upon the northwest corner of town in order to draw the attention of Major Foster's men away from the larger concealed attack from the west. With the battle plan in place, the Confederate forces waited and rested anxiously in the ranks.

Many of the troops were raw recruits whose only prior experience in firing a musket had been shooting game in the woods, not men in the streets. As many as 1,500, or, one-half of the rebel troops, were comprised of these recent additions to the Confederate ranks. These men were also ill-equipped, and many were unarmed. They had enlisted with the unrealistic belief that muskets would be issued to them.

Many of the new Confederate troops were fearful of attacking Lone Jack. To help assuage their fears, Jackman gave a rousing speech during those early morning hours. He warned his boys that there were about 1,000 Federal cavalry in Lone Jack with two pieces of artillery. He further cautioned them that the Union troops were well-armed, well-mounted with good horses, and under the command of an imposing leader. *"Men, I feel that we are going to have a hard fight of it, as the enemy is commanded by a very resolute officer. They have come out from Lexington in search of Quantrill and his band of braves, and they know full well it will take men of extraordinary nerve to cope with Captain Quantrill anywhere in Jackson County, and especially the Sni Hill."*[19] He

---

[19] Eakin, Joanne Chiles. *Battle of Lone Jack, August 16, 1862.* (Independence, Mo.: Two Trails Publishing, 2001), 35.

47

encouraged his soldiers to fight with the resolve of victory. He poetically reminded them to revenge the evilness and maliciousness that the Kansas Red Legs and Jayhawkers had inflicted upon their many mothers, wives and sisters. The speech was inspirational to those gathered and even to those who may have questioned the propriety of the attack.

With the Confederate battle plan prepared and with their troops properly encouraged, it was only a matter of a few hours before the break of daylight and the commencement of the battle in the streets of Lone Jack.

The Battle in the Streets of Lone Jack
August 16, 1862

At daylight, Federal pickets came in and reported that the enemy was advancing, about 3,000 strong. Major Foster ordered his men into line to await further instructions. About 40 minutes later, the attack would ensue.

The rebels' forces under Hunter, Jackman and Tracy in accordance with their prearranged battle plan had ridden towards the outskirts of the cornfield west of Lone Jack, and then dismounted. The men then anxiously assembled and awaited orders to begin their stealth advance. Hays formed his 400 mounted men in line to make his feint attack upon the northwest section of the town. To the right of Hays, Cockrell and his men were aligned in three columns awaiting Hays to make his move. According to Harrison Troy, their arms were as varied as their uniforms. It was to be a duel in which each man carried the weapon he could best handle.[20]

Cockrell's forces, with the sun now beginning to shine in their eyes, waited for Hays to make his advance from the northwest. For unspecified reasons, Hays failed to do so. Their patience was growing thin and despite Hays' failure to take the stage, Cockrell, after meeting with his company commanders, chose to move forward. He ordered the columns to proceed

[20] Burch, J. P. *A True Story of Chas. W. Quantrill And his Guerrilla Band.* (Vega, Tx.: n.p., 1923), 88.

through the cornfield still hoping to attack an unsuspecting Union force.

It is said that someone within their ranks while venturing into the cornfield accidentally discharged his musket and the Union forces were instantly in motion and their bugle sounded the men to arms.

The rebel plan for secrecy had been compromised and the Confederates in a wild rush dashed to the fences in the rear of the buildings in the village. From that moment on a desperate fight lasting four to five hours was waged throughout the streets of Lone Jack.[21]

By 6:30 a.m., the battle became widespread and general. The rebel forces attempted to turn both the right and left flanks of Foster's men; but, they were unable to do so by reason of a thick hedge, which protected each flank and afforded some protection to Foster's front. The rear of Foster's troops was well protected by a small, deep stream.

The initial assault upon the Union line became disorganized. Confederates were greatly confused by the hedge row, and tragically annoyed by Foster's sharpshooters. This compelled them into retreat where they rejoined the main body at the Anderson Grove about one mile from town. Once reformed, the Confederates advanced once again. Each man had only been allotted about six rounds of ammunition and had been ordered to preserve their charges as reasonably as possible under the circumstances.

As the battle intensified, the Confederate ammunition was running precariously low. There are reports of how 18-year-old Cole Younger had heroically ridden through Hays' ranks dispensing ammunition to the men.[22]

In the immediate front of the approaching Confederate troops were the two Union cannons. Although the battery inflicted damage to the advancing rebels, they continued pouring into the

---

[21] After the Battle of Lone Jack, Major Foster discounted the story that the fight began over an inadvertent discharge of a musket by a Confederate troop. It was his contention that it was one of his federal pickets who had sounded the warning and discharged the first round that morning.
[22] Younger, Coleman. *The Story of Cole Younger By Himself.* 1996 edition, 26.

town. The Federal troops soon began to fall back.

Hays, whose men entered the battlefield late and dismounted, noticed some confusion within the Union ranks. He saw soldiers attempting to shield themselves by their horses. Hays suddenly ordered his men to shoot the horses, and for many minutes more horses fell than Union soldiers. As the horses neighed and groaned in pain, Hays' men quickly charged the Federal battery.

Develin then re-appeared, much to Foster's dismay, and came onto the field rushing among his men and ordering them to fall back, which they did, abandoning the cannons. Seeing this, the rebels rallied and made an attempt to capture the artillery. One hysterical and foolhardy Confederate soldier leaped upon one of the cannons and began waving his slouch hat in victory. His celebration was short-lived as he was promptly shot and killed.

Sixty men including Major Foster charged the Confederates as they converged upon the Union battery. Foster and his men were able to successfully re-capture the cannons by repulsing the rebel forces by "inflicting terrible slaughter upon them." While in the act of dragging one of the cannons, Major Foster was shot and collapsed on the battlefield.

Captain H. M. Brawner, Company A, 7th Cavalry Missouri Volunteers, then assumed command of the Federal forces.

Seeing Major Foster down, his younger brother, Captain Melville Foster, rushed to his aid. As Captain Foster was making efforts to remove Major Foster from the field, a bullet ripped into his right breast. Despite the severe wound, he valiantly dragged his brother to the safety of the nearby blacksmith shop. There the semi-conscious Major and his gravely wounded brother remained throughout the balance of the conflict. According to Captain Brawner, 48 of Foster's men were wounded or killed in the fight to re-capture the two cannons.

The battle raged from one end of the town to the other. Despite the yellow banner waving from the Cave House signaling its use as a hospital, it had served another purpose as well. A few Federal troops had taken refuge in and around the hotel and other structures. This afforded them much needed protection and strengthened their firepower against the advancing Confederates.

The streets of the town, hedgerow and matured cornfield had become enveloped with smoke from the cannons, muskets and revolver fire like fog over a morning harbor. Soldiers on both sides

had difficulty seeing through the thick haze. Only the flag of the United States, which was whirling from the redoubt of the Cave House, was visible. Hays wanted the yellow hospital banner and Union flag from the rooftop destroyed. His men were suffering from those protected behind the hotel walls. Two or three of Hays' boys volunteered. They went forward gathering combustibles, and in a few minutes the hotel was ablaze. Mrs. Cave, the hotel's hostess, was compelled to evacuate the building. She promptly gathered her three small children and ran to the cornfield where she was inadvertently shot in the chest. Nothing would remain of the hotel but its charred ruins.

There was no skirmishing at long distance at any time during the battle. The bloody fighting took place in the street, only 60-feet wide. There was severe hand-to-hand combat, which lasted about a half an hour.

After more than four hours, Confederate forces gave way and retreated, leaving Union troops in command of the field . . . and their cannons. However, about the same time, Coffee came in sight with his reinforcements. Coffee had finally managed to collect his men after they had been scattered the previous night.

Brawner, realizing the precarious position of his men and facing concerns over the overwhelming advance of additional enemy forces, including the guerrillas under Quantrill, elected to withdraw from the field. Before doing so, he had his men spike one of the cannons before falling back. He had no alternative but to leave their two cannons behind, as there were no horses left to remove them.

Sometime later, the reinforced Confederate Army came up the blood stained street and took possession of the two cannons the

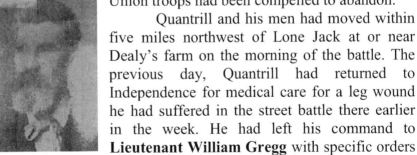

Union troops had been compelled to abandon.

Quantrill and his men had moved within five miles northwest of Lone Jack at or near Dealy's farm on the morning of the battle. The previous day, Quantrill had returned to Independence for medical care for a leg wound he had suffered in the street battle there earlier in the week. He had left his command to **Lieutenant William Gregg** with specific orders not to break camp under any circumstances. While Gregg and his men could hear the echoing sound of battle, they remained impatiently encamped. After the engagement intensified, Gregg could no longer restrain his men and they mounted their horses and sped towards the battlefield. They made it to Lone Jack around 10 a.m. as the final bullets were being fired. Quantrill's raiders played no active role in the battle. However, their approach was sufficient enough reason for Brawner to realize that standing to fight further was not in his army's best interest.

BLOOD ON THE STREETS

CHAPTER VII

Stark Realities

The Battle of Lone Jack left a ghastly spectacle in the town. Nearly every house and structure had been converted into a hospital or morgue. The losses on both sides were pronounced. Following the battle, the charred remains of two Union soldiers, one Confederate and one horse were found in the smoldering embers of the destroyed Cave House.

According to Captain Brawner, nearly every officer in the Union army, including himself, was either wounded or killed. He estimated their loss at 43 dead, 154 wounded and 75 missing in action. His estimate of the number of Union dead was overly conservative. Their true mortality rate was extremely higher. The report of the Federal casualties was more accurately reflected in the *New York Daily Tribune* on August 21. The *Tribune* gave the Union totals as 150 killed and wounded. It was even speculated that Major Foster and his brother had been mortally injured. In the end, it was determined that only Captain Foster, who had heroically saved the life of his commander and brother, had been so slain.[23]

During the evening hours following the Battle, Confederate troops were confronted with the daunting task of tending to the wounded and burying the dead.

---

[23] The legend surrounding U.S. Marshal Reuben J. "Rooster" Cogburn, made famous by the movie, *True Grit* (portrayed by John Wayne in 1969, which earned him a Best Actor award, and by Jeff Bridges in 2010, which earned him a Best Actor nomination) began at the Battle of Lone Jack. It was during the battle that Rooster had reportedly lost one eye.

Dr. Caleb Winfrey had formed a company of Lone Jack citizens, including James Noel, and they had enlisted under the command of Colonel Upton Hays only a few weeks earlier naming Dr. Winfrey as captain of the company. As a physician and elected captain, Winfrey felt and experienced the practical fall-out from the battle. During the onslaught, he had led two charges against Union troops who had occupied his home. Following the engagement, it became his demoralizing duty to care for his fallen comrades. Other citizens of Lone Jack soon followed Captain Winfrey into the town. They had slowly returned to explore the tragedy that had befallen their small community. Confederate soldiers led several mothers, wives, and other relatives through the buildings, street and fields to identify loved ones who had been slain or mortally wounded.

Inside the blacksmith's shop, captured Major Foster and his mortally felled brother were provided minimal medical attention. They anguished in pain and struggled to conceal the money they possessed. Major Foster had about $700 dollars hidden on him while Captain Foster had about $300 dollars. Their apprehension and worries intensified when several of Quantrill's guerillas, about a dozen in all, entered the blacksmith shop. Their mission was to ensure that Major Foster and his brother would not recover from their injuries. **Cole Younger** quickly thwarted their grizzly purpose. As the guerillas were threatening to kill the two brothers, Lt. Younger rushed into the room and promptly seized the assailants and had them summarily removed. Later, Major Foster reported that Younger took into his possession the money he and his brother had, along with their revolvers. Younger then made certain that they were delivered to their mother in Warrensburg.[24]

The dead were buried in two mass graves under the old lone black jack oak tree. In all there were 119 Federals buried in one grave and 47 rebels laid to rest in the other. The Confederate dead were wrapped in blankets and lowered into the east trench side-by-side with their heads facing west. The Federal soldiers were buried in the west trench with their heads and feet alternating close together. It is speculated that the large disparity of the number of Union to Confederate buried in the two graves is accounted for by the numerous family members of the fallen southern troops who had returned to the town to claim their dead.

In all, the casualty rate for Major Foster's men was nearly 40%. While the exact numbers may never be determined, there were 118 rebels purportedly killed; but, the full extent of their wounded was never fully

---

[24] Cole Younger years later related how he had intervened to save the life of Major Foster after he had fallen into the hands of guerillas. See, *The Story of Cole Younger By Himself.* Originally published in 1903. 1996 Edition, 26. This heroic act garnered Foster's respect and appreciation for Younger. During the period of some 25 years while Younger was incarcerated in prison in Minnesota following the Northfield Raid in 1876, Major Foster spent several of those years as an unrelenting advocate and supporter of Younger attempting to have the man who had saved him from death in the blacksmith shop in Lone Jack on the night of August 16, 1862, freed and paroled from prison.

ascertained. Noah Hunt, a resident of Lone Jack, claimed he counted 110 dead horses.

Soldiers and horses were not the only victims of the battle through the streets and structures of Lone Jack. Although the mistress of the Cave House, Lucinda Cave, had escaped with her young children while her husband's hotel was engulfed in flames, the breast wound she suffered in the cornfield was fatal; she died a few weeks later.[25]

---

[25] On the eve of the 75th commemoration of the Battle of Lone Jack in 1937, Cave's son, Jesse M. Cave, then 80-years-old and living at 3918 Holmes Street, Kansas City, Missouri, spoke to an *Independence Examiner* reporter about the morning his mother was fatally shot during the battle. At the time, Jesse was 5 years-old, when he, his mother and siblings were asleep in the Cave Hotel "when the firing began in the streets nearby about 6 o'clock." The article continued: *"A number of Federal soldiers broke into the hotel, and began firing out of the doors and windows at the Confederates who responded with a terrific assault. While the conflict was raging, the house, a two-story frame, began to burn. Seeing nothing but certain death if they remained inside, Mrs. Cave decided to face the possibility of fleeing from the house. She and her children did so, and, unhurt, made their way to a place of comparative safety a short distance west of the hotel, crouching down close to the ground, where they were hidden by tall weeds. One of the children, an infant in arms, clamored to be nursed. Jesse was one of the children huddled around her. 'I remember it all as if it had happened only yesterday,' Jesse Cave remarked.... 'Mother sat up and was reaching for my little sister, when a minie [sic.] ball struck mother in the breast. As soon as possible she was given treatment, but she never recovered, and three weeks later she died. None of the rest of us were injured. The baby died a few years later. One of the other children, my brother, William Henry Cave, was with us when it happened. He was 10 years old then and is still living, at the age of 85, at Everett, Wash[ington].'"* Independence Examiner, 14 Aug 1937. Jesse Cave died the following year in March 1938.

Other townspeople were left as widows or orphans as Captain Winfrey's company had consisted of residents from Lone Jack, many of whom had fallen during the fight. Numerous other civilians were also touched by the four- to five-hour blood bath through the streets of Lone Jack. Upon returning to town, they discovered the carnage, slaughter and bloodshed. Many of their businesses and homes had been either damaged or destroyed in the fight.

The Confederate victory was only a short-term gain. They were forced to retreat the following morning when Union troops under Colonel Warren approached the town from the south. Blunt's army was known to be on the move from Fort Scott on the west. According to Major Foster, Colonel Cockrell had personally told him that the rebel troops were completely out of ammunition. Without ammo and facing overwhelming forces, Cockrell and his Confederate Army were compelled to relinquish the town to the advancing Federal troops. This left the bulk of the burial detail to the remaining citizens of Lone Jack.

Confederate and guerilla forces following the Battle of Lone Jack dispersed in various directions. The large majority of the rebels withdrew and retreated towards Arkansas.

Quantrill and his band of guerillas remained behind in Jackson County to continue to harass Union patrols for the next couple of months before traveling south for the winter.

Hays and his battalion, including Winfrey, who was promoted to Major after the battle, and his company, remained in Missouri and moved southwest of Jackson County and away from the advancing columns of Union forces approaching Lone Jack.[26]

---

[26] Captain Winfrey went on to fight for the Confederate cause. He was with Colonel Upton Hays when Hays was killed near Newtonia. Thereafter, he became senior surgeon of Jo Shelby's brigade, and was present at the battles of Cane Hill, Prairie Grove, Champion Hill and

Gravesite of Upton Hays and other Confederates, Forest Hill Cemetery, Kansas City, Missouri

Upton Hays' days were numbered. In a skirmish with Union troops near Newtonia in southwest Missouri on September 13, Hays was instantly killed when a bullet penetrated his head while he had been leading a charge in attempt to drive-back Union pickets from Wisconsin. At the time of his death, Hays was wearing a large silk Confederate Flag that he had sewed into the lining of his frockcoat. The flag had been made and presented to him by the ladies of Westport at the outset of the War.

As to Cole Younger, it is uncertain whether he

---

the Second Battle of Springfield (January 8, 1863). He remained in Springfield, Missouri, after the Confederates withdrew in order to care for the wounded. He then became a prisoner of war and was sent to City Point, Virginia, until he was exchanged. After his release from City Point, he rejoined his command, and arrived at Vicksburg just prior to the siege. After the fall of Vicksburg in July 1863, he joined General Sterling Price and served as surgeon during Price's great raid into Missouri in the fall of 1864. He saw action at the Battle of Westport in Jackson County in October 1864, and after that battle, he remained to care for the wounded and dying. After the War, he returned to the practice of medicine in Pleasant Hill, Missouri, where he continued to practice into the early 1900s. In 1913, at the age of 90, Winfrey had an office in the Junction Building at 9th Street between Main and Delaware. Pages from his family Bible are archived in the Jackson County Historical Society's Archives.

retreated south with Hays or remained in Jackson County and joined Quantrill and his guerrillas after the battle. There is no question that Younger's war years began at Independence and Lone Jack. Soon, Cole's brothers, along with Frank James, and later Jesse James, joined him as members of Quantrill's raiders. The guerilla activities the Younger and James brothers learned as young men during the remaining years of the Civil War served as a training ground for their outlaw years that followed the War of the Rebellion.

It can be said that the Battle of Lone Jack was nothing more than a continuation of the Battle of Independence only five days earlier, and had served as the climax of the Confederate recruiting expedition into Jackson County.

The battles in the streets of Independence and Lone Jack were on-going segues to more unrest, turmoil, strife and heartbreak that would continue to plague Jackson County for the better part of the next three years, 1863-1865.

These conflicts were also only a foreshadowing of more horror, dismay, turmoil and tragedy that would befall the county.

Some historians have described the Civil War in Jackson County as a 30-years war that began on May 30, 1854, when the Kansas-Nebraska Act became law, and

did not conclude until Frank James was acquitted in 1884 for the final time by the law.

What is undisputed is that the outpouring of blood on the streets of Independence and Lone Jack brought the grief, terror and reality of the Civil War directly to Jackson County during those hot summer days and nights of August 1862. There would be many more heartbreaking and anguishing years to follow.

APPENDIX A

August 11, 1862: Action at Independence

The following are the official Union reports of the Battles of Independence and Lone Jack as compiled in the *Official Records of the War of the Rebellion*:

REPORTS.
Numbers 1. Brigadier General James Totten.
Numbers 2. Lieut. Colonel James T. Buel, 7th Missouri Cavalry.
Numbers 3. Capt. Jacob Axline, 2nd Battalion Missouri Cavalry.

Numbers 1. Report of Brigadier General James Totten.

HEADQUARTERS CENTRAL DIVISION OF MISSOURI,
Jefferson City, August 13, 1862.

COLONEL: Below are telegrams relative to the capture of Independence, received at this office on the 12th:
LEXINGTON, MO., August 12, 1862.

Brigadier-General TOTTEN:
Two hundred and forty men that I sent yesterday to Independence, under Major Bredett, have just returned, and report that Independence was attacked by 1,500 men, under a Colonel Hughes and Quantrill, and after four hours' hard fighting Lieutenant-Colonel Buel surrendered. It is reported that the rebels are marching on this place. Major McKee has not yet arrived. I shall telegraph Colonel Catherwood to send me two or three companies. I am very anxious in regard to Major Linder, of Harrisonville, with his two companies. He must be on the march to Independence.

DANL. HUSTON, Jr.,
Colonel, Commanding Post

BLOOD ON THE STREETS

LEXINGTON, MO., August 12, 1862.

General TOTTEN:
Are there any other men except Catherwood's on the way to this post? Cannot 200 arms get sent me by Catherwood's men? I have heard that Buel's men are all paroled.

DANL. HUSTON, Jr.,
Colonel, Commanding Post.

LEXINGTON, August 12, 1862.

General TOTTEN:
"Warner" has not arrived. Colonel Newgent, with his command, except 45 men, who took the dispatch the Major Linder, ordering him to Independence. I have 750 men, all told, at this post. Major McKee has not been heard from. Have sent an express for him. I would like to have Catherwood send all the men he can spare. There are 200 enrolled militia included in the 750. The enemy are reported 1,500 strong and constantly increasing in number. Major Bredett with his command, 200 strong, got within 8 miles of Independence, when he heard of the surrender and returned. I have just heard that Colonel Buel was surprised at 5 o'clock in the morning. It is a report, however.

DANL. HUSTON, Jr.,
Colonel, Commanding Post.

LEXINGTON, August 12, 1862.

General TOTTEN:
I have just received information from Independence. Colonel Buel was taken in the bank building after it had been set on fire. Our men fought them four hours. Captain Thomas, Missouri State Militia, was taken out and murdered after the surrender.
DANL. HUSTON, Jr.,
Colonel, Commanding Post.

The above is all the official information we have received in relation to the above. General Schofield has been informed of all the particulars in the case.

Very respectfully, your obedient servant,
JAS. TOTTEN,
Brigadier-General, Commanding Division.
Lieutenant Colonel C. W. MARSH,
Assistant Adjutant-General, Saint Louis, Mo.

Numbers 2. Report of Lieutenant Colonel James T. Buel, 7th Missouri Cavalry

SAINT LOUIS, MO., August 17, 1862.

SIR: I have the honor to report that the military post of Independence, Mo., was attacked on the morning of August 11, at daybreak, by the rebel forces under command of Colonel J. T. Hughes, numbering, from the estimate of officers of my command, from 700 to 800 men. These forces entered the town at two points, viz, by the Harrisonville road. The party entering by the Big Spring road divided into two parties, one of which attacked the provost guard, of 24 men, stationed at the jail; the other attacking the bank building, which was occupied as headquarters; also the armory of the Volunteer Militia, situated on the opposite side of the street, guarded by a detachment of 21 men, 16 of this number being Volunteer Militia. The main body, entering by the Harrisonville road, proceeded along the Big Spring road and the two streets leading to the camp, which was situated nearly 80 rods from the bank building, attacking the camp on the east and north sides, and thus cutting me off from all communication with the camp.

The first attack was made upon that part of the camp held by the company of Captain Thomas, Second Battalion Cavalry, and Missouri State Militia. This company, not being able to maintain its ground and being hard pressed, fell back to the cover of a stone wall running parallel with the south side of

65

the camp. The remaining companies, which were posted to the right and rear of this company, fell back to the same position, when, being enfiladed by a destructive fire, they retired along the stone wall, thus avoiding a galling flank fire from the enemy posted in a corn field. At this critical moment Lieutenant Herington , of the Second Battalion Cavalry, Missouri State Militia, was detached, with 65 men, to open, if possible, a communication with headquarters. Advancing northward, he was attacked by a superior force, which compelled him to seek the cover of a brick house, where he defended himself in a most gallant manner until he was apprised that further defense was useless, when he withdrew his command to Kansas City.

While Lieutenant Herington was performing this gallant action Captain Breckenridge, Seventh Missouri Volunteer Cavalry, senior office in the camp, tearing a piece of his shirt, raised it as a token of surrender. It was immediately pulled down by the men of his command. He persisted in doing this a number of times. From Lieutenant Meryhew, provost marshal, I learned that he, concluding that the bank building and camp had been captured and that our forces were retreating from the town, withdrew from the rear of the jail into the woods, making his retreat to Kansas City.

At 7 a. m. I concluded, from the fact that firing around the jail had ceased, that the provost guard had been captured. However, expecting the arrival of Major Linder I had resolved to hold our as long as possible. The rebels having gained possession of a brick house commanding the bank building kept up an incessant fire on it until nearly 9 a.m.

Having taken an officer prisoner, I learned from him that the troops were commanded by Colonel G. W. Thompson, who had succeeded to the command, Colonel Hughes being killed. The house adjoining the bank building having been set on fire, which in a few minutes would extend to the building of which I had possession, I communicated with Colonel Thompson by means of a flag of truce, asking an interview. At the interview which took place the following terms of capitulation were agreed upon, viz: The officers and men of my command were to be considered prisoners of war, the property and persons of the Union citizens to be respected; which terms were fully carried out by the rebel authorities.

My command on the morning of the 11th consisted of 312 effective men. The pickets on the Big Spring road were found dead. The pickets on the Harrisonville road are missing. Numbers of the men escaped in small parties thus leaving the number paroled about 150 men. I had no opportunity of getting the exact number, as numbers of them, as soon as paroled, left for Kansas.

Considering the conduct of Captain Breckenridge, above mentioned, as deserving of punishment, I ordered him under arrest, and he is now as such at Benton Barracks. Captain Cochran, Second Battalion Cavalry, Missouri State Militia, also acted in a cowardly manner, having hid himself in a cellar early in the action. I intended placing him under arrest also, but he left for Kansas.

The number killed and those who have since died of their wounds number 26. The wounded number 30, comprising First Lieutenant Vance and Second Lieutenant Pence, both of the Seventh Missouri Cavalry, who conducted themselves in a most gallant manner. Second Lieutenant Young and Second Lieutenant Swan also behaved gallantly. The loss of the enemy could not be ascertained, as early in the action they commenced carrying off their dead into the country. From authentic sources I learned that Colonel Hughes, Captain Clark, and the notorious Kit Chiles were buried at Independence. Among the wounded of the enemy were Colonel Thompson, Lieutenant-Colonel Boyd (fatally), and Major Wortle.

Respectfully submitted.
J. T. BUEL,
Lieutenant-Colonel Seventh Missouri Volunteer Cavalry[27]

---

[27] O.R. Series 1, Vol. XIII, Part 1, pp. 226-228.

Numbers 3. Report of Captain Jacob Axline, 2nd Battalion Missouri Cavalry (Militia)

SAINT LOUIS, August 26, 1862.

On Sunday, August 10, I received an order from Captain Loring, commanding post at Kansas City, to move immediately with my command, without baggage, to Independence, and report to Lieutenant-Colonel Buel, of that post.

I took with me my second lieutenant, Goss, and 63 men, non-commissioned officers and privates, and arrived at Independence a little after dark, and reported in person with my command to Colonel Buel, and was ordered by him to place my men on the south side of the camp ground. We tied our horses to the rail fence and slept behind them on the open ground. We were permitted to remain quiet during the night, but were aroused at daylight by firing, which commenced first near Colonel Buel's headquarters, distant about three-quarters of a mile from the camp. In the course of two or three minutes a very heavy and destructive fire was opened by the enemy on the north side of the camp and was returned with great spirit by the men as they emerged from their tents. I immediately formed my men on the first alarm and ordered them to advance toward the north of the camp and started, but was immediately assailed by a heavy fire from the east and another from the southeast; and seeing the men retreating very rapidly from the ground to the northwest corner and taking shelter behind a rock fence and many of them passing west along the fence out of the range of the enemy's guns, I ordered my men to direct their fire on the force on the east and southeast and gain the rock fence. The move was made with great firmness under a very destructive fire, which was returned with steadiness. The enemy was repulsed and we gained the position. In this charge we sustained a loss of 6 killed and 8 or 10 wounded.

Being still exposed to a steady fire from a concealed enemy in front and rear, we moved down the fence to the southwest corner of the camp ground. Here the rock fence crossed a gutter form 3 to 4 feet deep, where I posted my men, with some others who had rallied to us, and, while this move was being executed, Lieutenant Herington , of Company E, Missouri State Militia, came to my assistance. From this position we could protect our front and flanks and cover three-fourths of the camp with our fire. Shortly after gaining our position it was told us that some distance west of us a white flag was hoisted on the rock fence. Lieutenant Herington hurried to the place. I left the men in charge of Sergeant Blake and followed Herington west to collect and bring up the men who had scattered in that direction. After proceeding some 400 yards I met Captain Breckenridge, with a white cloth tied to a gun-stick. He asked me if he should hoist it. I told him certainly not; that if he did it would be at his peril. I here discovered that a large number of men were collected at a house still farther west, distant more than half a mile from camp. It was arranged that Lieutenant Herington should go there and collect a force of 50 or 60 men and move up the street north of the camp. The move was successfully made. I at the same time sent out 20 men under a sergeant to clear the ground and corn patches on the south side of the rock fence, which was done, and I, with the balance of the men, returned to the southwest corner of the camp ground, where Blake still held his position, though badly wounded, and 1 man killed in the last charge made. As soon as I arrived there some of my men went on the camp ground and brought 2,000 rounds of cartridges and distributed them to the men and we had determined to move forward in three detachments to the public square and take the town, but just at this time I was told that a white flag was approaching, and was asked by someone if he should fire upon it. I ordered the men not to fire, and sent a messenger to meet it and report to me their errand. As my messenger returned 4 men came up to where my command was posted and unfurled a white flag. This flag was borne by two of the enemy, and was accompanied by Captain Breckenridge and Adjutant Preble. Adjutant Preble said he was ordered by Colonel Buel to notify me that he had surrendered and that I was to surrender. I replied that Colonel Buel was not in command, and that I would not surrender. Captain Breckenridge then ordered those of his men who were with me to lay down their arms, which they did. I was then assured that we were surrounded by a force 700 strong. I was left with less than 75 men, who were fatigued with near four hours' hard fighting, and our strength and position fully known to the enemy. I saw that we were thus completely placed in their power, without a hope of further success. I reluctantly consented to surrender, and ordered my men to do so, under promise that the private property of the officers and men should be respected.

We lost 7 in killed and 12 wounded and many others left the field with bullet-marks in their clothes. My men had fought bravely. They had paid for their horses and saddles. They had repulsed five different charges of the enemy. Not a horse of theirs had been taken by the enemy, and many of the guns, that had told so truly on the rebels, were thus quickly turned over to them, and the guns that stopped the charge of Yager and Hughes are both in their possession, but the owners who used them are here.

Colonel Buel was taken prisoner three-fourths of a mile from the camp at his office. I received no order form him during the day except the order to surrender. Captain Thomas, of Company E, Missouri State Militia, was taken prisoner at his family residence, about a mile from camp, and shot by the enemy. Captain Cochran, I am told, at the first fire took shelter in a private house, and remained there till the fight was over. Lieutenant Goss, of my company, slept in the house of Corporal Miller. They started for the camp. Miller was killed, and Goss succeeded in escaping, but could not reach his command.

Lieutenant Herington , when notified of Buel's surrender and receiving the order to do so himself, quietly left, and brought his men and arms to the city. The enemy behaved themselves very orderly toward us after our surrender, for which they have my acknowledgments.

JACOB AXLINE,
Captain Company B, Second Batt. Cav., Mo. S. M.[28]

---

[28] O.R. Series 1, Vol. XIII, Part 1, pp. 229-230.

APPENDIX B

AUGUST 16, 1862: Action at Lone Jack, Missouri

SEDALIA, August 19, 1862.
Brigadier General JOHN M. SCHOFIELD:
Colonel Huston telegraphs this morning as follows:

General Blunt and Colonel Warren joined near Lone Jack, 4,000 men, sixteen pieces of artillery; had a severe fight yesterday, result unknown, within 10 miles of Lone Jack. Information by a flag of truce sent for our wounded. One of Colonel Warren's officers came into Lone Jack and our lieutenant conversed with him before fight.

JAS. TOTTEN,
Brigadier-General, Commanding Division.[29]

REPORTS.
Numbers 1. Brig. Gen. James G. Blunt, U. S. Army.
Numbers 2. Maj. Wyllis C. Ransom, 6th Kansas Cavalry.
Numbers 3. Capt. Milton H. Brawner, 7th Missouri Cavalry.
Numbers 4. Maj. Emory S. Foster, 7th Missouri Cavalry.

Numbers 1. Report of Brig. Gen. James 0. Blunt, U. S. Army.

FAYETTEVILLE, Mo., August 20, 1862.

SIR: Your dispatch of the 18th is just received. I came upon the united forces of Coffee, Hunter, Tracy, Jackson, and Cockrell, numbering 4,000, at Lone Jack, about 7 p. m. on the 17th instant.
On the morning of the 16th the rebel forces attacked Major Foster at Lone Jack with 600 State Militia, defeating him and capturing two pieces of artillery. The loss on each side was

---

[29] O.R. Series 1, Vol. XXV, p. 584.

about 50 killed and 75 to 100 wounded. Among the latter was Major Foster. Fosters command made a gallant fight, and were only defeated by overwhelming force.

On my arrival at Lone Jack I found General Warren, with a command of 800, consisting of the First Missouri and First Iowa Cavalry and two pieces of artillery, threatened with immediate attack by the whole rebel force, the rebel pickets being then in front of his camp but on hearing of my approach they immediately commenced a retreat under cover of the night availing themselves of the shelter of heavy timber for a distance of 6 miles, crossed our trail in the, and made a precipitate flight south. They have never halted since they commenced their retreat except long enough to feed their horses, and they crossed the Osage at this point yesterday at 10 a. m. My advance, under Colonel Cloud, skirmished with their rear guard yesterday, killing and wounding several and taking a number of prisoners.

Coffee is talking of forming a junction with Rains at Greenfleld and make a stand, which I hope they may do, as my command is much exhausted by forced marches and the stock is badly used up. Since I left Fort Scott my command has marched over 200 miles, on an average of 40 miles per day, without tents, and the last two days without subsistence, except as we could forage off the enemy; yet the men have borne their fatigue and privations cheerfully in anticipation of meeting the enemy. I arrived here at 2 o'clock this morning and shall march in an hour for Greenfleld.

JAS. G. BLUNT,
Brigadier-General, Commanding.
Col. E. C. CATHERWOOD2
Commanding, Sedalia, Mo.[30]

---

[30] O.R. Series 1, Vol. XIII, Part 1, pp. 235-236.

Numbers 2. Report of Maj. Wyllis C. Ransom, 6th Kansas Cavalry.

KANSAS CITY, Mo., August 17, 1862.

GENERAL: A body of United States troops, some 800 strong, were surprised yesterday morning by the rebel forces of Colonels Coffee, and Quantrill, and after a heavy resistance they were obliged to surrender with great loss. Our troops had a battery of two pieces,
which is now in possession of the enemy. From all appearances the enemy is moving on to Lexington. Large forces of our troops are moving toward the latter place from north of the river and from Sedalia.

In order to keep the enemy from retreating back, though, it will be necessary to throw a heavy force in their rear.

I have the honor, general, to be your most obedient servant,

W. C. RANSOM,
  Major Sixth Kansas, Commanding Kansas City.
Brig. Gen. BLUNT,
  Commanding Department of Kansas[31]

Numbers 3. Report of Capt. Milton H. Brawner, 7th Missouri Cavalry.

CAMP POWELL,
Lexington, Mo., August 20, 1862.

Sir: I have the honor to report that the forces sent out by your order, under command of Maj. Emory S. Foster, Seventh Regiment of Cavalry, Missouri State Militia, consisting of detachments from five companies of the Seventh Cavalry, Missouri Volunteers; three companies of the Sixth Cavalry, Missouri State Militia; two companies of the Eighth Cavalry, Missouri State Militia, and three companies of the Second

---

[31] O.R. Series 1, Vol. XIII, Part 1, pp. 236.

73

Battalion of Cavalry, Missouri State Militia, together with a section of two pieces of the Third Indiana Battery, in all 800 men, marched on the 15th instant to Lone Jack, 32 miles southwest of this place, arriving there about 9 o'clock same evening.

I, having ascertained, immediately upon arriving there, that about 800 rebels, under the command of Colonel Coffee, were encamped about 1 mile south of the town, we prepared against a surprise. The artillery was brought into position, commanding the lane through which we were passing, while skirmishers were thrown out on each flank and to the front, and the whole column moved forward. After advancing about three-fourths of a mile, between the town and the camp of the enemy, their cavalry charged down the lane upon us, but were received with a volley of musketry, which scattered them in all directions. Their camp was at the same time shelled by the battery with good effect. The enemy having fled, and no further demonstrations on their part being anticipated, the command returned to Lone Jack, arriving at 11 o'clock, and encamped for the night. On the morning of the 16th, about daylight, we were attacked by an entirely different force, commanded by Cockrell, Thompson, Hays, Quantrill, and others, numbering about 3,200, who, as we afterward learned, had been encamped about 9 miles northwest of Lone Jack. They came upon us under cover of corn fields and ridge fences, pouring upon us a most deadly fire, to which we replied with spirit. Our battery of two guns, supported by Company A, Seventh Cavalry, Missouri Volunteers, opened upon them with terrible effect, scattering them in confusion. They rallied, however, supported by overwhelming numbers. The battery was taken, but we retook it. Again it was lost and retaken. The contest at this time was terrible. Two-thirds of the detachment supporting the battery and 24 of the 36 men belonging to it are reported among the killed and wounded.

During one of the charges, made to recapture the battery Major Foster was dangerously wounded, and the command devolved upon me. The struggle was continued for nearly five hours, our men fighting gallantly during the whole time against vastly superior numbers, as well as better position on their part. Two parties having been detached the day before, our forces did not amount to more than 720 men. Nearly every officer of the command, including myself was either killed or wounded. The enemy was finally driven from his position, and the hard-fought field was ours. At this juncture the force under Coffee, whom we had repulsed the evening before, again appeared on our left flank, with the evident design of surrounding our worn-out troops and cutting off all retreat. The men, being utterly exhausted, and our ammunition almost gone, I deemed it unadvisable to hold the ground longer, and accordingly got the command together and marched off in good order toward this post, unmolested by the enemy.

We were forced, much to our regret, to leave the battery behind, the horses attached to it having all been killed and the harness mostly destroyed and other portions of the equipage scattered in all directions. The gallantry of the men was conspicuously displayed after the last recapture of the battery, they being forced to handle the guns entirely without the aid of horses. No horses could be obtained to draw the gun from the field, and we spiked one of them and otherwise very much injured the other, while the ammunition belonging to them was mostly destroyed before we left. The command arrived at this post on the same evening at 7 o'clock.

I take great pleasure in mentioning the courage and good conduct generally displayed by the men of the command. Among those deserving special mention for gallant conduct were Capt. H. P. Spellman, First Lient. Charles R. Combs, and Orderly Sergt. John P. Anderson, Company C; Lient. Robert D. Anderson, Company A; Lieutenant [Samuel M.] Baker, Company I, and Lieutenant [John] Schee, of Company E, Seventh Cavalry, Missouri Volunteers, and Captain [William W.] Owens and the officers and men of the Eighth Cavalry, Missouri State Militia; Asst. Surg. W. Cundiff, Second Battalion Cavalry, Missouri State Militia, also deserves special mention for gallant conduct and faithful performance of his duty while on the field. Sergt. J. C. Updegraff, of the Third Indiana Battery, displayed great gallantry and good conduct.

Our loss is, killed, 43; wounded, 154; missing, 75. Total, 272. The enemy acknowledged a loss of 118 killed. The number of their wounded is not definitely known, but undoubtedly much exceeds that of the killed. Of those reported missing at the close of the action numbers are returning daily, materially diminishing our loss.

I am, very respectfully, your obedient servant,

M. I. [sic.] BRAWNER,
  Captain Company A, Seventh Cavalry, Missouri
Volunteers.
Col. DANIEL Huston, Jr.,
  Seventh Cavalry, Mo. Vols., Comdg. Sub. Div., Central Mo.[32]

__Numbers 4. Report of Maj. Emory S. Foster, 7th Missouri Cavalry (Militia).__

GREENFIELD, May 1, 1863.

GENERAL: I have the honor to report that, in obedience to an order from you dated Jefferson City, August 12, 1862, I proceeded from Syracuse; to Sedalia, to take command of forces about to march to Lexington. Company H, Seventh Missouri State Militia, Captain [Elias] Slocum, from Syracuse, reported at 11 o'clock p. m. on the 12th. The two companies of the Eighth Missouri State Militia, Captains [Henry D.] Moore and Owens, and a section of the Third Indiana Battery, Lieutenant [J. S.] Develin, marching by rail from Jefferson, reported at 4 o'clock a. m. August 13. I marched immediately, and reached Lexington August 14 at 11 a in., a distance of 60 miles; men and horses very much worn-out, having marched forty-eight hours without food or rest.

I received an order from you at 1 o'clock a. m. August 15 to march at daylight in the direction of Lone Jack, with 800 men. At daylight I marched with a force consisting of detachments from five companies, Seventh Cavalry, Missouri Volunteers, three companies Sixth Cavalry, Missouri State Militia, two companies Eighth Cavalry, Missouri State Militia, three companies Second Battalion Cavalry, Missouri State

---

[32] O.R. Series 1, Vol. XIII, Part 1, pp. 236-238.

Militia, and one company Seventh Cavalry, Missouri State
Militia, together with a section of the Third Indiana Battery. In
consequence of a jealousy in regard to rank no field officers
were sent with me, as you directed should be done.

I marched directly for Lone Jack. About noon I
reported to Colonel Huston, commanding at Lexington, that the
enemy, 1,600 strong, were at Lone Jack, under Coffee, and that I
would fight that evening. We surprised the camp about 9 o'clock
that evening and completely routed the enemy. Lieutenant
Develin, being drunk, acted very badly, and was arrested, and the
artillery placed in charge of Sergeant [James M.] Scott.

The men then slept in line in Lone Jack. About
daylight the pickets came in and reported that the enemy was
advancing, about 3,000 strong. Several scouts had reported, and
no word from Warren, who should have been in supporting
distance. Two parties were still out, leaving us about 740 men.
Knowing the instructions you had given Colonel Warren, and
believing him to be in hearing of my artillery, I awaited the
enemy. The attack was made about forty minutes after the
pickets came in. The enemy attempted to turn both my right and
left, but were unable to do so by reason of a thick hedge, which
protected us on each flank and afforded some protection to our
front, our rear being protected by a small, deep stream, the
crossing of which we held. The enemy cavalry being thrown into
confusion by the hedge and annoyed by sharpshooters placed
behind it fled in confusion, rejoining the main body, which then
attacked us in front.

After a desperate fight of four hours duration the
enemy began to fall back. At this time Lieutenant Develin came
onto the field, and rushing among his men ordered them to fall
back, which they did, leaving the guns. Seeing this, the enemy
rallied and made an attempt to capture the artillery, but were
repulsed with terrible slaughter. Of 60 men led by me in this
charge only I reached the guns, and they were all wounded. In
the act of dragging the cannon out of the enemy's reach I was
shot down.

Captain Brawner was then in command. After a severe
hand-to hand fight, which lasted about a half hour, the enemy
gave way and retreated, leaving us the field and the guns. At this

time Coffee came in sight with about 1,500 men, having collected his forces, which were scattered the night before. Captain Brawner fell back, leaving the guns. About an hour after the enemy came up and took possession of the field. The fact that 740 men fought five hours against such odds and whipped them is sufficient evidence of the stuff of which they were made. They need no praise from me. Where all fought so well it is impossible to designate those most worthy of mention. Braver men never fought. Had your orders been obeyed the whole force of the enemy would have been captured or terribly routed and destroyed.

Colonel Warren came up the next morning after the fight and was in sight of the enemy all day. I was told by officers on the ground that general Blunt came up during the day, but no engagement took place. The enemy retreated south as soon as night came. I was told by Cockrell, who commanded the rebels in the fight that they were completely out of ammunition, which fact I stated to Colonel Warren. I can give no list of casualties, as the company commanders have not reported to me.

I am, general, your obedient servant,

EMORY S. FOSTER,
Major Seventh Cavalry, Missouri State Militia.
Brig. Gen. JAMES TOTTEN[33]

---

[33] O.R. Series 1, Vol. XIII, Part 1, pp. 238-240.

BIBLIOGRAPHY

Books

Barton, O.S. *Three Years With Quantrill A True Story Told by His Scout John McCorkle*. (Norman, Ok.: University of Oklahoma Press, 1992).

Burch, J. P. *Charles W. Quantrell : A True History of His Guerrilla Warfare on the Missouri and Kansas Border During the Civil War of 1861-1865.* (Vega, Tx.: J. P. Burch, 1923).

Brownlee, Richard S. *Gray Ghosts of the Confederacy*. (Baton Rouge, La.: Louisiana State University, 2011).

Eakin, Joanne Chiles. *Battle of Independence, August 11, 1862*. (Independence, Mo.: Two Trails Publishing, 2000).

Eakin, Joanne Chiles. *Recollections of Quantrill's Guerrillas*. (Independence, Mo.: Two Trails Publishing, 1996).

Eakin, Joanne Chiles. *The Blue & Grey Chronicle, 1997-2002*. (August 1997): 1:2. (Independence, Mo.: Two Trails Publishing, 2002).

Ehrlich, Nancy M. *August 11, 1862, First Battle of Independence, Missouri An Urban Confrontation*. (Independence, Mo.: Nancy M. Ehrlich, 2012).

Goodrich, Thomas. *Black Flag: Guerrilla Warfare on the Western Border, 1861-1865*. (Bloomington, In.: Indiana University Press, 1999).

Hale, Donald, R. *We Rode With Quantrill*. (Independence, Mo.: Blue and Gray Book Shoppe, 1982).

Jackson, David W., and Paul Kirkman. *LOCKDOWN: Outlaws, Lawmen & Frontier Justice in Jackson County, Missouri.* Sixth Edition. (Independence, Mo.: Jackson County Historical Society, 2012).

Jewett, Tom, ed. *Failed Ambition: The Civil War Journals and Letters of Cavalryman Homer Harris Jewett.* First Battle of Independence Commemorative Edition. (Lightning Source, Inc., 2012).

Journal and Proceedings of the Missouri State Convention. (St. Louis: George Knapp & Co. 1861).

Leslie, Edward E. *The Devil Knows How to Ride.* (New York: Random House, 1996).

Lotspeich, Cyrus B. *Personal experiences of C. B. Lotspeich, 1861-1865.* (n.p.: Cyrus B. Lotspeich, 1912).

Matthews, Matt, and Kip Lindberg. "Shot All to Pieces, The Battle of Lone Jack, Missouri, August 16, 1862." *North & South* (January 2004): 7:1.

Monaghan, Jay. *Civil War on the Western Border.* (Lincoln, Ne.: University of Nebraska Press, 1955).

Peterson, Norma, L. *Freedom and Franchise, The Political Career of B. Gratz Brown.* (Columbia, Mo.: University of Missouri Press, 1965).

Phillips, Christopher. *Damned Yankee: The Life of General Nathaniel Lyon.* (Baton Rouge, La.: Louisiana State Press, 1996).

Phillips, Christopher. *Missouri's Confederate, Claiborne Fox Jackson and the Creation of the Southern Identity in the Border West.* (Columbia, Mo.: University Missouri Press, 2000).

Siddali, Silvana R. *Missouri's War, The Civil War in Documents*. (Athens, Oh.: Ohio University Press, 2009).

Tenny, Luman Harris. *The War Diary of Luman Harris Tenney*. Unpublished manuscript.

War of the Rebellion, The: A Compilation of the Official Records of the Union and Confederate Armies. O.R. Series 1, Vol. XIII, Part 1.(Washington, D.C.: Washington Government Printing Office, 1880).

Wallace, William. *Speeches and Writings*. (Kansas City, Mo.: The Western Baptist Publishing Co., 1914).

Webb, W.L. *Battles and Biographies of Missourians or The Civil War Period of Our State*. Originally published in 1901. (Springfield, Mo.: Oak Hills Publishing, 1999).

Wilcox, Pearl. *Jackson County Pioneers*. (Independence, Mo.: Jackson County Historical Society, 1990).

Union Historical Company. *The History of Jackson Co., Missouri*. 1966 indexed edition. (Kansas City, Mo.: Union Historical Company, 1881).

Younger, Cole. *The Story of Cole Younger, By Himself*. Originally published 1903. (Springfield, Mo.: Oak Hills Publishing, 1996).

Newspapers

Independence Examiner, 14 Aug 1937.
Kansas City Daily Journal of Commerce, various dates.
Kansas City Star, 26 Jan. 1913.
Kansas City Times, 16 Aug. 1938.
Liberty Tribune, 15 Aug 1862.
Liberty Tribune, 22 Aug 1862.
Liberty Tribune, 29 Aug 1862.
New York Daily Tribune, 21 Aug 1862.

BLOOD ON THE STREETS

<u>**Internet Resources**</u>

http://ebooks.library.cornell.edu/m/moawar/text/waro0019.txt (viewed 12 Sep 2012).

http://www.archives.gov/research/alic/reference/military/civil-war-armies-records.html (viewed 12 Sep 2012).

http://www.archive.org/stream/warrebellionaco17offigoog#page/n4/mode/2up (viewed 12 Sep 2012).

http://www.civilwarhome.com/records.htm (viewed 12 Sep 2012)

http://www.historiclonejack.org/museum.html
.

INDEX

ILLUSTRATIONS

2 Abraham Lincoln, President of the United States, three-quarter length portrait, seated, facing right. Courtesy Library of Congress Prints and Photographs Division Washington, D.C. LC-DIG-ppmsca-19470 (digital file from original neg.).

3 Claiborne Fox Jackson. Courtesy Wilson's Creek National Battlefield, *WICR 11499*, as viewed at http://www.civilwarvirtualmuseum.org/1861-1862/12th-confederate-state/claiborne-jackson.php.

10 James Henry Lane (1814-1866), politician and leader of the Free State Party of Kansas, full-length portrait, with gun. Courtesy Library of Congress Prints and Photographs Division Washington, D.C. LC-DIG-ppmsca-11516 (digital file from original item, front).

11 Jemison's [sic] Jayhawkers. Courtesy Library of Congress Prints and Photographs Division Washington, D.C. LC-USZ62-100061 (b&w film copy neg.).

12 George Caleb Bingham. Jackson County Historical Society Archives. JCHS004007L.

15 Colonel Upton Hays. Jackson County Historical Society Archives, Watts Hays Collection, gift of Marian Franklin. JCHS020499L.

17 General Joseph Orville "Jo" Shelby. Jackson County Historical Society Archives. JCHS008875M.

18 Fort Union, 1861. Whitney, Carrie Westlake. *Kansas City, Missouri: Its History and Its People, 1808-1908.*

Volume 1. (Chicago: S. J. Clarke Publishing Company, 1908), 201.

19 William Clarke Quantrill. Portrait in charcoal on paper, which was prominently displayed in a frame for years at Quantrill reunions. Jackson County Historical Society Archives.JCHS009241XXX.

22 Thomas Coleman "Cole" Younger. Anon.

23 Henry Washington Younger. Jackson County Historical Society Archives. JCHS003403S.

24 General Samuel D. Lucas. From an original oil painting in the custody of the Jackson County Historical Society Archives. JCHS000554L.

25 John T. Hughes. Jackson County Historical Society Archives. JCHS007766M.

26 Gideon W. Thompson. Jackson County Historical Society Archives. JCHS007767M.

27 Bird's Eye View, Independence, Missouri. Cropped. From an original engraving in the custody of the Jackson County Historical Society Archives, Gift of Mrs. Edwin L. Gustafson. JCHS022618XXX.

29 William McCoy residence. Jackson County Historical Society Archives. JCHS001406MB.

30 1859 Jackson County Jail. From the *Illustrated Historical Atlas, Jackson County, Missouri*. 1877. Reprint. (Independence, Mo.: Jackson County Historical Society, 2007). JCHS011133L.

31 Southern Bank; later McCoy Bank. Buel's headquarters during the First Battle of Independence. Jackson County Historical Society Archives. William J. "Bill" and Annette W. Curtis Collection. JCHS016011M.

34 John Taylor Hughes memorial tombstone, Woodlawn Cemetery. Jackson County Historical Society Archives. JCHS008744M.

39 1853 plat for the land where the Battle of Lone Jack would be fought in 1862. The plat for the official town of Lone Jack (to the north of this location) was filed in 1841. Jackson County Recorder of Deeds. Plat of Easley and Winfrey Addition, 1853.

46 Soldiers at Lone Jack army encampment at one of the annual picnics held there each August. Undated photograph. Jackson County Historical Society Archives. Gift of Donald R. Hale. JCHS022727SC. Also used on the cover.

50 Stereograph showing some of the 65 horses of the 9th Massachusetts Battery of Light Artillery killed during the Battle of Gettysburg lying in Trossel's barnyard. Courtesy Library of Congress Prints and Photographs Division Washington, D.C. LC-DIG-stereo-1s02537 (digital file from original stereograph, front).

51 The Confederates charged again to drive the Union soldiers from the two cannons. "Missourians Stages a Private Fight in Deadly Battle of Lone Jack," *Kansas City Star*, 16 Aug 1938. Image by F. Miller. Also used on the cover.

52 William Gregg. From a zinc printing plate from the *Independence Examiner.* Jackson County Historical Society Archives. JCHS013247S.

56 Dr. Caleb Winfrey. "Shelby's Senior Surgeon at 90: He Visits His Office in the Junction Building Every Day," *Kansas City Star*, 26 Jan. 1913.

57 Thomas Coleman "Cole" Younger in his later years. Cropped. Jackson County Historical Society Archives. JCHS000922L.

58 Tombstone of John Owen, husband of G. E. Owen, who died at the Battle of Lone Jack. Lone Jack Cemetery. Jackson County Historical Society Archives. JCHS005522M.

60 In Memory of Our Confederate Dead, Forest Hill Cemetery, Kansas City, Missouri, 1904. This image was taken in 1904 by Margaret M. (Franklin) MacPherson, a granddaughter of Colonel Upton Hays and Margaret J. (Watts) Hays. Jackson County Historical Society Archives, Watts Hays Collection, gift of Marian Franklin. JCHS022916S.

61 Battle of Lone Jack Civil War monument. Lone Jack Cemetery. Jackson County Historical Society Archives. JCHS022728M.

62 Battle of Lone Jack historical marker. Jackson County Historical Society Archives. JCHS005521M.

ACKNOWLEDGEMENTS

The Jackson County Historical Society continues its mission to preserve and promote local history, and should be commended. Wise readers who support this nonprofit, historical organization also deserve high marks.

Specifically, I would like to thank David W. Jackson, Archives Director for the Jackson County Historical Society, for assistance both in contributing historical details included in this commemorative booklet, and also for designing and putting the finishing touches to this product.

Others whose welcomed contributions have proven helpful include: Sharon Snyder, Nancy Ehrlich, Joanne Eakin, and Tom Jewett, author of *Failed Ambition,* which made available the diary and writings of his ancestor, Homer Jewett.

I would also like to thank those who participated in the Civil War Sesquicentennial living history event sponsored by the Jackson County Historical Society that re-created on August 11, 2012, the 1862 assault on the 1859 Jackson County Jail: Ralph A. Monaco, II; Gregg Higginbotham; Jim Beckner; Gina Sifers; David Bears; Steve Hall; Joe W. Hudgens; Bill Stilley; Dan Stilley; Jay Jackson; Dan Hadley; Bob Eckhoff; Aaron J. Racine; Bob Talbot; Keith Fangman; Joann Barber; Barbara Jackson; Brad Pace; Belinda Canaday; and, Derek Kraus.

And, congratulations to the Lone Jack Historical Society for their efforts in presenting a weekend of activities commemorating the 150th Anniversary of the Battle of Lone Jack on August 16 and 17, 2012. Their dedicated Board of Directors are: Alinda M. Miller, President and Webmaster of historiclonejack.org; Dan Hadley, Vice President; Linda Barta, Secretary; Dan

BLOOD ON THE STREETS

Enlow; Betty Williams; Paul Clum; David Goodman; and Kathy Smith. A special thanks goes to Steve and Jodie Brown (for allowing their home to be converted to the Cave Hotel), and to Jim and Dianna Scalf (for providing parking and camping on their property across the road).

ABOUT THE AUTHOR

Ralph A. Monaco, II is a life-long resident of Raytown, Missouri. He graduated from Rockhurst University in 1978, *summa cum laude*, earning bachelor degrees in history and political science. In 1981, he received his law degree from the University of Missouri at Kansas City School of Law. He is a charter member of the Kansas City law firm, Monaco, Sanders, Gotfredson, Racine & Barber, L.C. He has been in the private practice of law for the last thirty-one years and he is a member of the Missouri Bar and the Western District of the Federal Court in Missouri. His peers in the legal community have recognized him for his legal work by issuing him an AV attorney rating.

Monaco has been active in the political, historical and civic communities in Jackson County. He formally served on the Raytown School Board, and served as School Board President. He was elected to the Missouri House of Representatives, District #49 in 1996 and went on to serve four terms, including serving as Chairman of the House Judiciary Committee. Currently, he is serving as the President of the Jackson County Historical Society. He has received numerous public service awards including the Acorn Lifetime Membership Award by the Missouri PTA, Missouri Judiciary Legislator of the Year Award, the Missouri Bar Legislator of the Year Award, the Association of Retarded Citizens of Missouri Friend of the ARC Legislator of the Year Award, the Outstanding Service Award from Jackson County Parks & Recreation, the Volunteer of the Year from Jackson County Parks & Recreation; Making History Come Alive Award from the Jackson County Historical Society, Lifetime Membership Award in the Raytown Historical Society, Pioneer of

Harrodsburg Award and membership in the Kentucky Colonels.

Monaco continues to remain very active with historical organizations and in historical portrayals. He has a passion for living history and Civil War reenacting. For well over 20 years, he has portrayed Abram Comingo, a 19th century attorney and U.S. Provost Marshal for the Sixth Congressional District during the Civil War. In addition, he has provided first person portrayals of other historical figures including Manuel de Lisa, a Spanish Fur Trader who helped outfit the Lewis & Clark Expedition; James Slover, Frank James' defense attorney; Edgar Allan Poe, the poet and master of the macabre; George Caleb Bingham, the Missouri artist and politician; Col. Thomas H. Swope, the philanthropist and purported murder victim at the hands of Dr. B. Hyde; and Jesse James, Jr., the son of the bandit Jesse James.

Monaco is the author of *The Strange Story of Col. Swope & Dr. Hyde* (Independence, Mo.: Two Trails Publishing, 2010); and, *Son of a Bandit: Jesse James and the Leeds Gang* (Kansas City, Mo.: Monaco Publishing, L.L.C., 2012).

Currently, he is working on his fourth, non-fiction book. He has also authored several manuscripts and historical retrial performances, including the retrials of Frank James, Dr. Hyde for the alleged murder of Col. Swope and Jesse James Jr.

He and his wife Karen live in Raytown, and they have two daughters, Lindsay and Lisa.

Made in the USA
Coppell, TX
08 November 2019

11163031R00057